PHILOXENIA

a seat at my table

PHILOXENIA

a seat at my table

KON & SIA KARAPANAGIOTIDIS

Hardie Grant

BOOKS

I dedicate this book to my late father, Leo, who taught me that hope and beauty can be found everywhere.

Contents

Welcome to my table

Welcome to *A Seat at My Table: Philoxenia*, a cookbook to be shared and passed on to loved ones, to bookmark, dog-ear and to scribble your cooking ideas and inspiration on. This is a cookbook that my mum, Sia, and I lovingly created to be enjoyed as part of your daily kitchen life. It's a celebration of growing and making your own food, of living sustainably, and of eating food that nurtures your body. It's a book with community at its centre.

Welcome to our home and kitchen table, a place where anyone can create something magical. Great food comes not from a recipe or how well you follow it but from our hearts, our curiosity, our creativity and from our desire to connect and experience intimacy and belonging with others. Great food creates space for us to be seen, to share, to laugh, to celebrate, to comfort, to care and simply to enjoy being together.

This cookbook is a celebration of filotimo, the foundation of Greek culture. It means being 'a friend of honour'; it is about the power and importance of love, kindness and generosity, and how we can experience and share this through food and enjoying a meal together. It is like breathing for us Greeks: to offer a helping hand, open the doors to our homes and provide a seat at the table for someone who needs it.

Alongside filotimo is philoxenia: being a friend to the stranger. It's about extending this kindness and generosity to the stranger in need of help and a place to rest. I truly believe food humanises us, tearing down walls of prejudice and fear, and creating a social scaffolding that allows us to embrace one another. I'm donating 100 per cent of my proceeds from this book to the Asylum Seeker Resource Centre (ASRC), and Hardie Grant is also generously donating $1 from each book sold. So when you invite people around your table to share a meal from this book, you are also creating a seat at the table for people seeking asylum.

I feel so honoured to be able to share these recipes with you, as well as the experience of creating this cookbook with my mum. When I suddenly lost my beautiful father, Leo, when I was 27, I had so many regrets about the stories never shared, the experiences we never had together, the things I never took the time to ask, and the culture and traditions I had lost with his passing. I wanted never to have that regret again. I wanted to celebrate my mum, my culture and my origins, and to protect them with all I have.

My parents taught me to show filotimo and philoxenia through food, as a way to open the door to our stories and culture. It is an invitation to be curious. So we hope you enjoy the journey and the food, as well as my mum's sustainability and cooking tips and my dad's gardening tips. May *A Seat at My Table* inspire you to share the connection and joy of breaking bread together.

In everything, there is a share of everything.
— ANAXAGORAS

About the recipes

In these pages, we'll explore how food can humanise us, transform and sustain communities, and act as a tool of resistance and activism. But let's start with the basics.

First, none of my recipes are referred to as indulgences or treats. Diet culture distorts our sense of self and our relationship to food.

Second, this book is for all of you, no matter your cooking skills, dietary needs or budget. All that matters is that you make these recipes with love, heart and fun. I want you to feel excited, curious and engaged when you are using this book, not as if you might be missing out or being excluded from any page or story. I want people who eat your food to say, 'Yia sta heria sas' – 'I kiss your hands' – celebrating your skill as a cook.

We are all capable of creating beautiful, nurturing food by embracing the 5 Ps: passion; play; patience; practice; and pragmatism. Cooking food from a culture that is new to you is meant to be fun. It's a chance to play and to do it with passion and curiosity. Bringing to it a mindset of patience and practice will allow you to enjoy the journey of trying new recipes without judgement or any pressure to get it 'right'. Finally, pragmatism will allow you to cook with what you have at home or can afford to source.

Let me guide you through a few key things to know about the recipes in this book.

- **Substitutes** There are many reasons you may want to substitute an ingredient – perhaps you have a different vegetable in abundance in your garden or on its last legs in the crisper, maybe you can't find the ingredient, are allergic to it or find it's not within your budget. These recipes are achievable with the ingredients you have available to you. After all, there are many paths to the same destination. That's where the Ingredient substitutes section (page 287) comes in.

- **Make it vegan** Every recipe in this book is either vegetarian or vegan. I want every dish to be accessible to vegans, so if the recipe is not yet vegan, you will see a note on the recipe page about how to make it vegan. There are more tips on vegan alternatives later in the book too (page 290).

- **Make it gluten-free** If a recipe isn't gluten-free, you'll find a note on the recipe page about ingredients to substitute or leave out to make it so.

- **Make it low FODMAP** I want this book to be inclusive for people with irritable bowel syndrome (IBS) and other digestive disorders. On page 293, you'll find a dedicated section on the high-FODMAP ingredients for which you can use substitutes to make a dish low FODMAP.

- **Nut allergies** Ninety-five per cent of the recipes in this book can be made nut-free. In savoury recipes, you can leave them out altogether and the dish will still sing. The challenge will be with just a handful of the sweet recipes – you can omit the nuts but unfortunately I can't promise they will taste as good.

- **What to do with leftovers** Like many of you, I am passionate about reducing food waste, so each recipe includes simple tips for leftovers. You can also check out Sia's guide for leftovers on page 282 and Leo's gardening tips on page 286.

- **Sustainability** I am passionate about sustainability and food security, so, wherever possible, this book will show you how to use every part of a vegetable or fruit – be it broccoli stems to make patties or basil stems to infuse oil – and how to compost whatever cannot be used. And there are even more sustainability tips on page 281!

- **Oven temperatures** Temperatures in this book are for conventional ovens. If using a fan-forced oven, reduce the temperature by 20°C (35°F).

- **Measurements** This book uses 20 ml (¾ fl oz) tablespoons; if you are using 15 ml (½ fl oz) tablespoons, be generous with your tablespoon measurements. Metric cup measurements are used, i.e. 250 ml (8½ fl oz) for 1 cup. In the US, 1 cup is 237 ml (8 fl oz), so American cooks should be generous with their cup measurements.

The Greek Pantry & Kitchen

How to make your own Greek kitchen basics

Mizithra

Lay a muslin cloth flat on a surface, pour 1 kg (2 lb 3 oz) Greek-style yoghurt into it, wrap up with a rubber band and hang off a tap overnight in a cool area to drain into a thick labneh. Then, place the labneh in a bowl and bury it in thick rock salt. Leave it in a cool place until it hardens into a thick, solid, salty Greek hard cheese ready for grating.

Olives

Gently bruise or crush each olive in a mortar and pestle or make 4 small slits in each olive. Place in a large bowl and cover with rock salt. Set aside for 2 weeks, changing the water after 1 week (this will get the bitterness out). Drain and transfer to an airtight jar or container and cover with a mixture of canola oil and vinegar. You can also add any of your favourite spices or aromatics, including garlic, chilli, rosemary, thyme, bay leaves, lemon zest or cardamom seeds.

Ricotta

Bring 4 litres (135 fl oz) full-cream milk to the boil in a large saucepan, then reduce to a simmer. Add 120 ml (4 fl oz) white vinegar and heat for 2–3 minutes, or until the milk curdles. Gently scoop out the curds with a slotted spoon and set aside to rest, or place in a colander to drain for a firmer ricotta.

Tomato paste

I recommend following my yiayia's method: cut tomatoes into quarters, then season well with salt and cover with a cloth. Then, break them down with a fork, transfer to a bottle and cover with olive oil.

Tomato sauce

Blanch tomatoes in a saucepan of boiling water, then set aside until cool enough to handle. Peel and grate flesh into a zip-lock bag and freeze until needed.

Yoghurt

Add 1 litre (34 fl oz/4 cups) milk to a saucepan over a medium heat and bring to the boil. Remove from heat and, while still warm, add 1 kg (2 lb 3 oz) Greek-style yoghurt. Cover and set aside overnight – this will double or triple the amount of yoghurt you started with.

Let food be thy medicine and medicine be thy food.
– HIPPOCRATES

The art of cooking with what you have

A common complaint about cookbooks is that often the recipes use ingredients quite different from what you actually have available to you, so let's address that.

Here are ways to make delicious vegan Greek food with any food you have in your kitchen.

Greek vegan vegetable roast

You can use this marinade with whatever vegetables you have in your fridge.

200 g (7 oz) tinned diced or crushed tomatoes
1 tablespoon tomato paste
1 teaspoon sweet paprika
1 teaspoon Greek oregano
salt and pepper, to taste
4 garlic cloves, finely diced
2 onions, finely diced
handful freshly chopped mint and/or parsley
125 ml (4 fl oz/½ cup) extra-virgin olive oil

Preheat the oven to 180°C (360°F). Prepare vegetables by peeling and dicing (depending on what you have) and place in a roasting dish. Combine these marinade ingredients and pour over the vegetables, mixing together with your hands. Bake until vegetables are tender and golden.

Greek vegan bean soup

Here's my recipe for a simple soup stock to which you can add any type of bean to create a delicious meal.

4 tablespoons extra-virgin olive oil
1 onion, diced
2 carrots, diced
2 celery sticks
3 cloves
2 bay leaves
1 vegetable stock cube
1 tablespoon tomato paste
200 g (7 oz) tinned diced or crushed tomatoes
salt and pepper, to taste

ANY OF THE FOLLOWING DRIED AND SOAKED OR BOILED BEANS OR LEGUMES:

chickpeas (garbanzos)
lentils
cannellini beans
butter (lima) beans
northern beans
red kidney beans

Sauté olive oil in a large pot with onion, carrots and celery until tender. Stir in cloves, bay leaves, vegetable stock cube and tomato paste. Season with pepper. Add tinned tomatoes and fill the saucepan to about three-quarters full with water. Add beans and simmer for at least 15 minutes, or until beans are tender. In the last 10 minutes of cooking, season with salt to taste.

Salt is born of the purest parents: the sun and the sea.
— PYTHAGORAS

Greek vegetarian or vegan pastry

If you have phyllo pastry, some eggs and any combination of cheese and vegetables, you can make a simple savoury Greek pastry. To make it vegan, leave out the eggs and use vegan substitutes for the dairy.

10 phyllo pastry sheets
butter or vegan butter, melted, or olive oil
feta or vegan feta
eggs, whisked

ANY CHOPPED OR GRATED GREENS OR VEGETABLES, SUCH AS:

spinach
silverbeet (Swiss chard)
endives
chicory
leek
spring onions (scallions)
grated zucchini (courgette)
butternut pumpkin (squash)

Preheat the oven to 180°C (360°F). Sauté vegetables in butter or olive oil until tender. Combine in a bowl with beaten egg.

Butter the base of a 30 cm (12 in) square baking tray and layer 5 sheets of phyllo over the base, buttering each one as you go. Pour in the egg mixture and finish with the 5 remaining phyllo sheets, buttering each as you layer them. Bake until crisp and golden.

Greek pasta bake

Pour béchamel sauce (see page 214) over any leftover pasta and sauce, toss through your favourite cheese and bake until golden.

Rice with greens

This is a tasty and crowd-pleasing side dish you can make simply with rice, onion and whatever greens you have available.

2 tablespoons extra-virgin olive oil
1 onion, diced
1 teaspoon sugar
200 g (7 oz/1 cup) long-grain rice
salt and pepper, to taste

ANY OF THE FOLLOWING CHOPPED GREENS:

leek
silverbeet (Swiss chard)
spinach
chicory
endives

Sauté onion with olive oil in a frying pan. Add greens and gently cook for a few minutes until wilted. Add rice, season with salt and pepper, and fry.

Anytime homemade dip

Tinned beans such as cannellini beans, chickpeas (garbanzos) or butter (lima) beans can make a delicious dip in minutes.

Drain and wash the beans, tossing into a blender with a good swig of extra-virgin olive oil and any chopped herbs you have to hand – mint, parsley, basil or dill. Add a generous squeeze of lemon juice, some roughly chopped garlic and season to taste with salt and pepper. Blend until the mixture reaches desired consistency – you may need to the add a little extra olive oil or water to loosen the dip if it's too chunky.

How to make your own mezedakia (mezze) platter

Greeks love to eat mezze, sampling and sharing a little bit of everything. It is something fun and simple you can do. There are literally dozens of different things you can add to your platter. No need to spend a fortune at a deli, you can make a beautiful mezze platter for yourself, your family and friends or a party of guests with these simple steps.

Make it colourful

Make your platter look beautiful by using lots of different-coloured vegetables, fruits and nuts to contrast. Choose a neutral platter, be it white or a wooden serving board.

It really is a mix and match experience that you can curate to your tastes, dietary needs and budget. Pick from any of the following iterations and the ones you and your friends and family enjoy.

Choose your vegetarian or vegan cheese

Thinly slice kasseri, kefalograviera, graviera, kefalotiri, manouri cheese, mizithra or cube some Greek feta, grill some halloumi, or make some saganaki bites using the kefalograviera or graviera.

Add some grilled or roasted vegetables

Sliced zucchini (courgette), pumpkin (winter squash), eggplant (aubergine), grilled or roasted capsicum (bell pepper), whole garlic cloves or artichokes dressed with a mixture of extra-virgin olive oil, chopped parsley, white wine vinegar and salt and pepper

Add some raw and pickled vegetables

Sliced celery and carrot sticks, strips of bell peppers, fennel and radishes or toursi, cucumbers and lemon wedges

Add some nuts

Walnuts, pistachios, sunflower seeds, almonds, cashews, pepitas (pumpkin seeds) and pine nuts

Add some small dip bowls

Tzatziki, melitzanosalata, tirokafteri, hummus, beetroot (beet) dip, spicy Greek feta dip, fava dip, skordalia, whipped Greek feta, labneh, butter bean dip, olive paste, garlic sauce and honey

Add some dairy if you like

Boiled eggs, Greek-style yoghurt, marinated Greek feta

Add fruits

Sliced melon, apricots, nectarines, cherries, watermelon, lemons, apples, peaches, grapes, mandarins, cherry tomatoes, rockmelon, persimmon, fresh figs, dates, prunes and dried figs

Add something a little more substantial

Fritters (dill, chickpea, onion, pumpkin/winter squash, zucchini/courgette, tomato, split pea, fennel), dolmades, pita bread, horta, eggplant (aubergine) and zucchini rolls with ricotta or feta, zucchini flowers, mini Greek pizzas, Greek tomato feta bites, Greek chips, lahanodolmades, halloumi chips, soutzoukakia, Greek feta balls, mini Greek omelette tarts, mini feta and zucchini quiches, spinach and feta puff pastry triangles, feta baked in phyllo and honey, pita chips

Add mini pastries

Halloumi/ricotta pastry cigars, halloumi skewers, tiropitakia, mini spanakopita triangles

Add fresh herbs and oils for colour and taste

Mint, basil, dill, Greek oregano, parsley, Greek extra-virgin olive oil

We should look for someone to eat and drink with before looking for something to eat and drink.
– EPICURUS

The world of Greek greens

In Greek culture we love our greens. Our lush, wondrous mountainous regions that are home to wild artichokes, asparagus and olive trees are also a sanctuary to more than 300 varieties of edible greens and herbs. We have a love affair with 'horta', as we call our greens. We love to boil them and enjoy them with olive oil and lemon, we love to fry them and make them into omelettes, add them to our salads with feta and tomatoes, and barbecue them on an open grill under coals or wood. We love to add them to our revithia stews (chickpeas) and, with feta, they are the star ingredients in our countless iterations of pita, the most famous being spanakopita.

The wilder the greens, the better. My mum will find the most divine wild greens anywhere and everywhere, be it in the countryside, on farms or on vacant urban blocks of land – we are people who love to forage! Make sure, however, to soak the found greens in water multiple times, and wash with care and boil them before using.

If they are sweet, odds are you can eat them raw like rocket (arugula). The uses for Greek greens are countless. You can:

Boil them Add vinegar and/or extra-virgin olive oil and some lemon, Greek oregano and salt. Add them to a salad or a casserole.

Eat them raw Just add them to salads with tomatoes, cucumbers, olives, feta, capsicums (bell peppers) or whatever you love.

Add them as filling They make a great filling for a pita, such as spanakopita.

Fry them Then add them to some beaten eggs and feta to make an omelette.

Examples of some Greek greens and how best to cook with them

The following greens can be boiled and added to salads with potatoes, zucchini (courgette), lemon, white vinegar, salt, pepper, olive oil and Greek oregano, or added to a vegan tomato-based stew with vegetables: zohos, vlita (amaranth), kardamo (shepherd's purse), vrouves (mustard greens), radiki (chicory/dandelion), rapini and beetroot (beet) leaves – boil for salads with Kafkalida (chervil), tsouknida (nettles), marathon (wild fennel) and vlita (amaranth) – these go great as a filling in Greek pastries like prasopita, spanakopita and hortopita.

Silverbeet (Swiss chard), tsouknida (nettles) and avronies (wild asparagus) can be fried as part of an omelette or added to a pastry, pita or fritter as a filling.

Radiki (chicory), sorrel, roka (rocket/arugula), myroni (shepherd's needles), endives, purslane can be eaten raw or added to salads with feta, olives, Greek oregano, olive oil, vinegar, sliced capsicum (bell pepper) and cucumbers.

You can find Greek greens such as zohos, rapini and vlita most commonly at Vietnamese and Chinese fresh vegetable shops and markets.

The mind is not a vessel to be filled but a fire to be kindled.
– PLUTARCH

The world of Greek pasta

There are dozens of varieties of Greek pasta, from rice-, shell- and square-shaped pastas, to coarse and crumb-like pastas, and thick, hollow pastas. The sauces that accompany them are diverse too, ranging from a simple topping of mizithra to a rich coating of a tomato- or cream-based sauce.

Here are some of the most popular Greek pastas that you can find at any Mediterranean deli.

Life is short, the art long.
– HIPPOCRATES

Orzo
A short-cut pasta that looks like a big grain of rice. Usually made with semolina, it goes beautifully in stews, casseroles and soups.

Hilopites
An ancient pasta that comes in both small squares and longer thin strips. Made with flour, eggs, milk and salt, hilopites are beautiful with mizithra, in a pasta soup or pasta bake.

Trahana
A coarse, crumb-like pasta. It's great in a soup with grated cheese or cooked in a thick tomato sauce. Trahana is one of the world's oldest foods.

Makarounes
Usually made with flour and water, it is rolled into small pasta shapes with one's finger when rolling out the dough, it goes beautifully with a thick tomato sauce or a butter-based sauce with mizithra.

Makaronia
A thick spaghetti made from durum wheat and semolina, fantastic on its own with grated mizithra or as the pasta filling for pastitso.

Skioufikto
A traditional Greek pasta handmade with wheat flour, salt, water and olive oil or butter. It has a cylindrical shape and it is perfect in burnt butter with chopped dill and capers with grated mizithra.

The world of Greek cheeses: an introduction to the greatest hits

Our love of cheese is best exemplified by the fact that the earliest recorded cheese in human history is Greek feta, a cheese as old as Homer's Odyssey. You will not find a Greek table without cheese on it. Our cheese obsession runs deep, with more than 60 varieties.

Kefalograviera

A wheel-shaped cheese made from ewe's milk or a mix of goat's and sheep's milk, famously known as saganaki once fried. Also a fantastic filling for vegetarian fritters or grated on top of any pasta.

Feta

Made with sheep's milk or a mix of sheep's and goat's milk, aged and stored in brine, feta is served as a side with every meal at the Greek table, while also going beautifully in everything from salads to pastries, and being crumbled on top of lathera dishes and fried with peppers, onions, garlic and tomatoes. If you can't find Greek feta, Bulgarian feta is a good substitute.

Kaseri

A semi-hard cheese made from sheep's milk, it's perfect in everything from a mezze platter with figs, melon and grapes, to salad sandwiches, to a filling for a spanakopita, prasopita or tiropita.

Mizithra

Made from pasteurised goat's or sheep's milk or a combination of both, it is the Greek parmesan but more salty and creamy. This white hard cheese is most commonly used as a cheese topping for pasta. If you can't find mizithra, you can use parmesan cheese instead.

Kefalotyri

A hard, salty cheese made from unpasteurised goat's or sheep's milk or a combination of both. It can be fried into a delicious saganaki, grated on pasta, added to a mezze platter or grated into your béchamel sauce or to finish your pastitso or moussaka.

Manouri

A semi-soft cheese made from sheep's or goat's milk, it is a great addition to salads with tomatoes, cucumbers and olives and pastries such as tiropitakia or tiropita. It is less salty than feta but creamier; you can even use it in cheese-based sweets.

Halloumi

Made from a mix of goat's and sheep's milk, this is a white, creamy and salty cheese that can be eaten as part of a mezze. It's also great fried, grilled or barbecued. Topped with a squeeze of lemon, it's also perfect grated over chips or pizza.

You will never do anything in this world without courage. It is the greatest quality of the mind next to honour.

– ARISTOTLE

Mezze & Small Dishes

ντολμάδες

Dolmades

SERVES 4

120 ml (4 fl oz) extra-virgin
olive oil, plus extra for
drizzling
2 small onions, finely diced
½ teaspoon sugar
200g (7 oz/1 cup) long-grain
rice, washed, drained and
patted dry
30 g (1 oz/½ cup) dill, finely
chopped
15 g (½ oz/½ cup) flat-leaf
(Italian) parsley, finely
chopped
10 g (¼ oz/½ cup) mint, finely
chopped
170 ml (5½ fl oz/⅔ cup) water
30 large silverbeet
(Swiss chard) leaves
salt and pepper, to taste
1 lemon, to serve

MAKE IT VEGAN
It already is!

MAKE IT GLUTEN-FREE
It already is!

WHAT TO DO WITH LEFTOVERS
Any leftover rice mixture can be
enjoyed as a meal on its own, or mixed
with egg, flour and breadcrumbs and
formed into rice patties to be baked or
fried. Leftover boiled silverbeet (Swiss
chard) can be chopped up to use in an
omelette or spanakopita filling.

In Ancient Greece, these heavenly parcels of goodness were
called thria and were made with tender fig leaves. Today,
most people who are familiar with dolmades know of them
as parcels of rice in vine leaves, but for me nothing beats
swapping out vine leaves for tender silverbeet (Swiss chard),
picked straight from the garden. You can also wrap them in
cabbage leaves and cover them in a gorgeous avgolemono
sauce – these are called lahanodolmades.

Heat 2 tablespoons of the olive oil in a frying pan over a medium
heat. Sauté onion and sugar for 2 minutes. Add rice, herbs and
water and cook for about 5 minutes until the rice is starting to
become like a pilaf. Season to taste with salt and pepper.

Bring a large saucepan of water to the boil. Add silverbeet
leaves and cook until soft and tender. Remove from the water
and lay on a tea towel to dry. Using a sharp knife, slice the leaves
off the stems and lay on a flat surface. Place 1 teaspoon of the
rice mixture at one end of a leaf and roll up like a cigar into
dolmades. If you have a leaf that is torn such that you cannot
make a dolmades from it, add another leaf over half of it and use
both to wrap the rice mixture in. Repeat with remaining leaves.
Don't wrap too tightly as the rice will expand when cooked.

Return silverbeet stems to a pot of boiling water, cook for
2 minutes and set aside.

Grease a large pot with 3 tablespoons of the oil and place
silverbeet stems in to cover the base. Now place the dolmades
in carefully (you want them to snuggle up next to each other,
leaving no room). Pour in just enough water to cover, drizzle with
remaining oil and the remaining juices and leftovers from the rice
mixture pot. Put a plate on top that covers the whole inside of the
pot so as to keep the dolmades in place for the first part of the
cooking process. Bring to the boil, then reduce to a simmer and
cook over a low heat for 20–25 minutes.

Remove the plate and cook for about another 15 minutes until
all the juices have evaporated. Gently remove the dolmades
and put on a serving plate. Squeeze over lemon and drizzle with
extra-virgin olive oil to serve.

Σαγανάκι

Saganaki | Fried cheese

MEZZE DISH

150 g (5½ oz/1 cup) plain
(all-purpose) flour
6 tablespoons canola oil
250 g (9 oz) kefalograviera
cheese, sliced
1 teaspoon Greek oregano
extra-virgin olive oil, to
drizzle
1 lemon, halved, plus extra
to serve (optional)

I could eat saganaki for breakfast, lunch and dinner – that first bite that you take straight out of the pan brings a rush of joy.

The term saganaki itself does not speak to a specific cheese. My recipe uses kefalograviera, as it's the cheese most commonly used, but firm Greek cheeses, such as kasseri, graviera, halloumi, manouri and kefalotyri, are also popular. The term saganaki refers to the type of dish prepared in a small frying pan. It is the root word of sagani, a frying pan with two handles, and is served in the same pan in which it is cooked.

Fill 1 large bowl with cold water and 1 small plate with the flour. Heat canola oil in a large frying pan until hot. Dip slices of cheese first in the water and then in the flour, shaking off any excess.

Cook, in batches, until golden on both sides. Set aside on a platter. Sprinkle with Greek oregano, drizzle with olive oil and squeeze over a lemon to serve.

MAKE IT VEGAN
Use a vegan kefalograviera cheese.

MAKE IT GLUTEN-FREE
Use a gluten-free flour.

WHAT TO DO WITH LEFTOVERS
Leftover kefalograviera works beautifully grated in omelettes, scrambled eggs, moussakas, pastitsos and toasted sandwiches.

Μπουγιουρντί

Feta saganaki

MEZZE DISH

120 ml (4 fl oz) extra-virgin
   olive oil
2 red onions, quartered
3 garlic cloves
1 green and 1 yellow capsicum
   (bell pepper), sliced
zest of 1 lemon
4 ripe tomatoes, diced
200 g (7 oz) Greek feta
2 teaspoons lemon thyme
5 g (⅛ oz/¼ cup) mint, finely
   chopped
15 g (½ oz/¼ cup) dill, finely
   chopped
1 tablespoon Greek oregano
   leaves (fresh or dried)
1 teaspoon dried chilli flakes
   (optional)
salt and pepper, to taste
crusty bread, to serve
lemon slices, to serve

This dish is the perfect representation of what I love about Greek cooking. It's truly a dish to share, made for placing right at the heart of your kitchen table with a fork for each guest so they can dig right in and grab some capsicums (bell peppers), onions, tomatoes and gooey feta all at once. You can cook a whole slab of Greek feta on top of your fried vegetables – enjoy scooping it up with a fork as it melts – or break it up into chunks all over your pan.

Heat oil in a large frying pan over a low heat.

Now we are going to add the rest of the ingredients in order of what takes the longest to cook.

Add the red onion and garlic and fry for 2 minutes.

Add capsicum and lemon zest and fry for a further 2 minutes.

Add tomato and fry for a further 5 minutes. Top with feta.

Add herbs and continue cooking for a few minutes until the feta softens. Add chilli, if using, and season with salt and pepper.

What you are looking for is a dish where all the vegetables are fried and golden, the tomato sauce is thick and the feta is starting to melt and is all soft and easy to break up with your fork. Serve with crusty bread and slices of lemon.

MAKE IT VEGAN

By just using a vegan Greek feta.

MAKE IT GLUTEN-FREE

It already is!

WHAT TO DO WITH LEFTOVERS

It's delicious spread on toast, or you can mash leftovers together with a fork to make a dip.

Τηγανιτή ελληνική φέτα με μέλι, δεντρολίβανο και θυμάρι

Pan-fried Greek feta with honey, rosemary and thyme

MEZZE DISH

1 egg, beaten
50 g (1¾ oz) plain
  (all-purpose) flour
200 g (7 oz) Greek feta slice
  (in a thick block)
120 ml (4 fl oz) extra-virgin
  olive oil
50 g (1¾ oz) honey
zest of 1 lemon, plus extra
  to serve
1 teaspoon lemon thyme,
  chopped, plus extra
  to serve
1 teaspoon chopped
  rosemary
25 g (1 oz) pistachios, crushed
1 tablespoon sesame seeds

Seeing the abomination known as 'fetta' trying to be passed off as Greek feta makes me furious. They are incomparable and simply a cynical financial move by multinationals to try to bypass the fact that feta has Protection Designation of Origin (PDO) status, as do iconic cheeses from France, Spain and Italy, for they are national treasures unique to their region.

Greek feta is particularly precious, for it is the oldest cheese in recorded human history. In Greek mythology Cyclops Polyphemus was said to have created the cheese by accident, and it is referenced in Homer's Odyssey, which dates back to the 8th century BC. We still preserve feta using the same brine technique as the Ancient Greeks did.

Today, no meal is complete without a slice of feta on the kitchen table. In fact, the word 'feta' means slice. It is a deeply entrenched part of the Greek national identity, way of life and history.

Fill 1 small bowl or shallow plate with cold water, 1 small bowl or shallow plate with beaten egg and another plate with the plain flour. First dip the block of feta in the cold water, then dip both sides in the beaten egg and then both sides in the plain flour.

Heat olive oil in a frying pan until hot. Add lemon zest and lemon thyme to the oil. Add the block of feta and cook on 1 side for 3–4 minutes, or until nice and golden brown, then turn and cook for a further 3–4 minutes, or until golden brown. Transfer to a paper towel to drain excess oil and leave for 2 minutes. Transfer to a serving plate and drizzle with honey, and sprinkle with pistachios, lemon zest, extra lemon thyme, rosemary and sesame seeds.

MAKE IT VEGAN

By using a vegan feta and leaving out the eggs, and by using maple, date or dandelion syrup, vegan honey or agave nectar instead of honey.

MAKE IT GLUTEN-FREE

By using gluten-free flour.

WHAT TO DO WITH LEFTOVERS

You can blend with some cream cheese and Greek-style yoghurt into a whipped feta dip.

Labneh με ρόδια και φιστίκια Αιγίνης

Labneh with pomegranates and pistachios

MEZZE DISH

1 kg (2 lb 3 oz) Greek-style
   yoghurt
¾ teaspoon salt
1 tablespoon chopped fresh
   mint
1 tablespoon chopped chives
4 tablespoons pomegranate
   seeds
50 g (1¾ oz) pistachios,
   crushed
3 tablespoons extra-virgin
   olive oil
1 tablespoon honey

Labneh is simply full-fat yoghurt drained overnight with a little salt, which drains the whey from the yoghurt and leaves you with a thick, spreadable cream, like cream cheese. It is beloved throughout the Middle East as much as it is in Greece. Labneh has a history spanning more than 2000 years and originates from the Levant region that includes modern-day Palestine and Syria.

I love the freshness of this dish and that you can drizzle anything you love on top of it. It's delicious with just a simple drizzling of olive oil, but you can also make it really special by serving it with anything from fresh mint, parsley, Greek oregano, basil or dill to crushed walnuts, pistachio nuts, pine nuts or slivered almonds, or lemon zest or honey.

Place the Greek-style yoghurt in the centre of a clean tea towel or muslin cloth and sprinkle with salt. Fold up the edges of the cloth and secure with a rubber band. Hang off a sink tap in a cool place overnight to drain into the sink.

Pick your favourite medium-sized serving platter or dish. Spread the labneh onto the dish, spreading it out using the back of a spoon. You don't need this to be perfect, just spread consistently and as you like.

Sprinkle with herbs, pomegranate seeds and crushed pistachios. Drizzle with the extra-virgin olive oil and honey to serve.

MAKE IT VEGAN

By using maple, date or dandelion syrup, vegan honey or agave nectar instead of honey, and by using a Greek-style soy, plant-based or coconut yoghurt.

MAKE IT GLUTEN-FREE

It already is!

WHAT TO DO WITH LEFTOVERS

When refrigerated, this will keep well for at least a few days. It's perfect to use as a dip, for spreading on your toast or as a filling for sandwiches, wraps and burgers.

Τσιπς χαλλουμιού

Halloumi chips

MEZZE DISH

500 g (1 lb 2 oz) halloumi
2 eggs, beaten
150 g (5½ oz/1 cup) plain (all-purpose) flour
100 g (3½ oz/1 cup) breadcrumbs
250 ml (8½ fl oz/1 cup) canola oil
90 g (3 oz) cherry tomatoes, halved
4 tablespoons Greek-style yoghurt
1 teaspoon za'atar or sumac
2 tablespoons tahini
1 tablespoon roughly chopped mint
2 tablespoons pomegranate molasses
1 lemon, quartered
4 tablespoons crushed pistachios
finely chopped mint, to serve

I do not have the space in this cookbook to share all my halloumi recipes but here are some tips to get the imagination going. Try filling little puff pastry cigars with halloumi and deep frying them. Or simply try frying large, thick slices of halloumi and finish with lemon, olive oil, mint and pomegranate seeds. Grated halloumi goes wonderfully on top of Greek fries. And finally, grilled halloumi goes beautifully in a roasted vegetable salad or even a fresh tomato, lettuce and onion salad.

Wrap your slab of halloumi in a tea towel or paper towel and set aside for 10 minutes (this will dry the halloumi so it cooks better). Slice it into whatever size you'd like your chips to be.

Place egg in one bowl, flour in a separate bowl and breadcrumbs in a third bowl. Dip each halloumi chip first in the egg, then the flour, then the breadcrumbs and transfer to a plate.

Fill a small–medium frying pan with enough canola oil to come 3 cm up the side of the pan. Add halloumi chips, in batches, and topping up the canola oil as the chips absorb the oil, and cook for about 2 minutes, or until golden. Take care not to overcrowd the pan otherwise the chips won't cook properly, and fry on each side until golden.

Transfer to a plate lined with a paper towel to absorb the excess oil. Transfer to a serving plate and arrange alongside cherry tomatoes.

Combine yoghurt, sumac or za'atar and tahini in a small bowl.

Serve halloumi chips with tahini dip, pomegranate molasses for drizzling and lemon wedges for squeezing over. Sprinkle with pistachios and mint.

MAKE IT VEGAN

By using a vegan halloumi and by using a Greek-style soy yoghurt, plant-based Greek-style yoghurt or coconut yoghurt and a vegan egg mix.

MAKE IT GLUTEN-FREE

Use gluten-free breadcrumbs and gluten-free flour.

WHAT TO DO WITH LEFTOVERS

The words 'halloumi' and 'leftovers' – never the twain shall meet.

ελιές ούζου

Ouzo olives

MEZZE DISH

120 ml (4 fl oz) extra-virgin
   olive oil
250 g (9 oz) Kalamata olives
zest of 1 lemon
3 bay leaves
2 sprigs fresh rosemary,
   leaves picked
4 cardamom seeds
50 ml (1¾ fl oz) ouzo

Watch you don't set yourself on fire when making these olives, as the pan flares up quite brilliantly when you add the ouzo! These are full of flavour and delicious eaten warm, straight from the pan, with bread for dipping in the juices. Yum!

It is the ouzo that makes this dish such a delight. Ouzo is an anise-infused spirit typically served in accompaniment with mezze, and is exclusively a product of Greece and Cyprus. The way to say cheers in Greek 'yamas' is short for 'stin iyia mas', which means 'to our health'.

Heat extra-virgin olive oil in a medium-sized pan over a low heat. Add olives, lemon zest, bay leaves, fresh rosemary and cardamom seeds. Slowly add the ouzo (make sure you are as far away as possible when you add it, as the pan will likely flare up). Cook for 3–4 minutes and serve.

MAKE IT VEGAN
It already is!

MAKE IT GLUTEN-FREE
It already is!

WHAT TO DO WITH LEFTOVERS
Bottle the olives with canola oil and white vinegar in a sealed bottle and these olives will last for a few months in your fridge.

Τηγανητά πατατάκια

Greek fried chips

MEZZE DISH

canola oil, for frying
4 large potatoes, quartered
   or sliced into thick chips
salt and pepper, to taste
1 teaspoon Greek oregano
50 g (1¾ oz) Greek feta,
   to garnish
lemon wedge, to garnish
   (optional)

I love making Greek chips; they honestly taste better than any other chips or fries I have eaten. The key to success is the technique used when frying them, namely making sure the canola oil is super hot first. Do not overfill your pot with chips, so they can actually fry properly, and once you have placed the potatoes in, do not touch them at all (no poking or mixing them up with a fork). That is how you get such perfect fried chips. The other key tip for a truly unique fries experience is to be generous with the salt, then sprinkle on the Greek oregano and feta, and squeeze the lemon over, if using.

Fill a large pot or saucepan with enough canola oil to come at least 10 cm (4 in) up the sides of the pan and heat until very hot. Add potatoes and cook, without moving around, for about 10 minutes, or until golden and crisp. Using a slotted spoon, remove from oil and transfer to a plate lined with paper towel. Sprinkle with salt and pepper, Greek oregano and feta to serve. You can also squeeze over some lemon juice.

MAKE IT VEGAN

Use a vegan feta or leave the feta out.

MAKE IT GLUTEN-FREE

It already is!

WHAT TO DO WITH LEFTOVERS

Thinly slice the leftover chips, warm up a frying pan with canola oil and place chips across the base of the pan. Crack beaten eggs over it and add some feta to make a delicious potato omelette.

Βίγκαν ελληνικά κεμπάμπς

Vegan kebabs

SERVES 6

250 g (9 oz) vegan halloumi, cut into cubes

2 zucchinis (courgettes), cut into thick slices

2 red onions, cut into wedges

250 g (9 oz) cherry tomatoes

1 green capsicum (bell pepper), deseeded and thickly sliced

MARINADE

200 ml (7 fl oz) extra-virgin olive oil

juice and zest of 1 lemon

1 bay leaf

4 garlic cloves, finely diced

a few thyme sprigs, leaves picked

2 sprigs rosemary, leaves picked

1 tablespoon Greek oregano

salt and pepper, to taste

A barbecue can be a very lonely place when you are a vegetarian. Like many other cultures, we Greeks love our meats and seafoods, from lamb on the spit to slowly cooked roasts filled with lots of garlic, fresh herbs and olive oil, to kebabs, prawns, and calamari, and octopus cooked in ouzo and finished with lemon and Greek oregano. I have countless memories of being told it was OK to eat a little lamb, beef or chicken and that it didn't count. I still remember uncles trying to convince me that lamb on the spit was vegetarian! Being an outlier at such a young age definitely builds resilience and teaches you to stick to your values no matter the pressure.

When I barbecue, I love cooking up halloumi, Greek greens, mushrooms, sweet capsicums (bell peppers) and eggplant (aubergine) to name but a few of my favourites. I love combining my favourite vegetables to make a vegetarian or vegan kebab, letting them luxuriate in a delicious Greek marinade for a few hours and then grilling them slowly.

Preheat the barbecue to hot.

To make the marinade, combine oil, lemon juice and zest, bay leaf, garlic, thyme, rosemary and Greek oregano in a small bowl and season to taste.

Toss halloumi and vegetables in the marinade and thread onto soaked wooden skewers.

Grill, turning and brushing with more marinade, for about 10 minutes, or until golden brown.

—

KON'S TIP: *If you are using wooden skewers, make sure to soak them in cold water for at least an hour beforehand to help prevent them from burning when you use them.*

MAKE IT VEGAN

It already is!

MAKE IT GLUTEN-FREE

It already is!

WHAT TO DO WITH LEFTOVERS

They go perfectly in a salad tossed with anything from tomatoes and cucumbers to cannellini beans, chickpeas or butter beans.

Πιπεριές

Piperies | Roasted peppers

MEZZE DISH

250 g (9 oz) green or red
    capsicums (sweet peppers)
170 ml (5½ fl oz/⅔ cup)
    extra-virgin olive oil
3 garlic cloves, diced
30 g (½ cup/1 oz) flat-leaf
    (Italian) parsley, chopped
seeds from ¼ pomegranate
salt and pepper, to taste

We have a love affair with capsicum (sweet peppers) in Greece – we love to roast and grill them, stuff them with rice and cheese, mash and puree them into delicious dips, top our Greek pizzas with them and pickle them as toursi.

This is a dish I have enjoyed so many times with my mum. We love roasting them and watching them get their beautiful brown colour. Sometimes we will eat them with the roasted skin, but you can take the skin off if you prefer.

After roasting, just place them in a plastic bag for one minute to help their skins naturally loosen and then, using your fingers, peel all the roasted skins back to reveal the delicious flesh.

Preheat the oven to 200°C (390°F) and line a baking tray with aluminium foil.

Pierce each of the capsicums about 6 times with a sharp knife (this will make them easier to cook) and toss in half the olive oil.

Place them on a prepared tray and roast for about 30 minutes, or until they are golden brown and soft.

Peel off the skins (as described above) or leave as is and place on a serving platter. Top with garlic, parsley, pomegranate seeds and season with salt and pepper. Drizzle over remaining olive oil to serve.

MAKE IT VEGAN
It already is!

MAKE IT GLUTEN-FREE
It already is!

WHAT TO DO WITH LEFTOVERS
So tasty as part of a topping for a pizza, or blend on their own or with Greek feta to make a delicious dip.

Κολοκυθοανθοί τηγανητοί γεμιστοί με κεφαλογραβιέρα

Fried zucchini flowers stuffed with kefalograviera

MEZZE DISH

50 g (1¾ oz) kefalograviera cheese
20 zucchini (courgette) flowers
150 g (5½ oz/1 cup) plain (all-purpose) flour
2 eggs, beaten
salt and pepper, to taste
canola oil, for frying

When they're in season, I love nothing more than picking the delicate flowers of the zucchini (courgette) in the early hours of the day as the warm weather inspires the flowers to open up. You can fill these magical little flowers with whatever your heart desires, from a delicious rice and herb mixture to goat's or feta cheese. As they were out of season when I wrote this book, I have gone for the 'battered with gooey, delicious cheese' option!

Cut the cheese into 20 small pieces that will fit into flowers. Place one piece of cheese into the centre of each flower and twist the tip of the flower to enclose. Set aside.

Prepare the batter by combining flour and eggs in a bowl. Gradually pour in enough water, while mixing, to achieve the consistency of thick cream. Season with salt and pepper.

Pour enough canola oil into a large frying pan or saucepan to come a few centimetres up the sides and heat until very hot. In batches, dip each zucchini flower into the batter, then straight into the hot oil and cook for 3 minutes, or until crisp and golden.

Set aside to drain on a paper towel and serve immediately.

MAKE IT VEGAN

Use a vegan kefalograviera cheese/vegan cheddar/gouda/halloumi cheese.

MAKE IT GLUTEN-FREE

Use a gluten-free plain flour.

WHAT TO DO WITH LEFTOVERS

They are so delicious there is no chance of leftovers!

LOVE

Greek food has its origin in thousands of years of history, storytelling, mythology, resistance, and family and community gatherings. Recipes are passed on from generation to generation and are celebrated. My recipes come proudly from my Greek parents' rich cultural and working class roots and they have a story that dates back thousands of years. Our food culture is part of the cradle of western civilisation itself.

The diples and loukoumades I will teach you to make are sweets that have been spoken of as far back as the 5th century BC in the comedies of Aristophanes, while the Greek olives I invite you to enjoy date back to Minoan times, growing in Crete in 2500 BC. For thousands of years, Greeks have savoured and feasted on the figs, cheeses, olive oil, barley, bread, chickpeas, honey, wild greens, olives and cucumbers that feature in so many of my recipes. Today I invite you to share in this story and be a custodian of our food culture too.

Since the days of antiquity, Greeks have made an art of welcoming the stranger, traveller or guest, no matter how distant the lands they have travelled from. We even have a Greek god, in Xenios Zeus, who is dedicated to being the protector of guests. It is part of our heritage, our DNA and our moral code.

Anyone who has ever visited a Greek home knows this spirit of welcome the moment they step through the door. Our home is your home. Our food is yours to share. You are treated like family because, once in our home sharing a meal, you are already part of our extended family. That is how deep the spirit of hospitality and welcome is for us.

Love is all we have, the only way that each can help the other.
— EURIPIDES

We also welcome and hold onto the spirit of philoxenia to this day because Greeks understand that we have simply won the lottery when it comes to being in the right place and time, and our freedom and safety is fragile. We know that with the change of the winds it could be us driven into the arms of danger, in need of sanctuary and welcome in the midnight hour, so we extend our welcome with open hearts without any expectation of reciprocity.

The Greek tavern is the best known public iteration of this in Australia. What draws people to it is the gathering, the dance, the joy, the connection to something bigger than yourself and foreign to you.

Just like the Greek tavern, every dish contained within this book is for sharing; there is no 'this is your plate and this one is mine' – there is only 'ours' at the Greek kitchen table. We cook to share, to experience all the tastes and flavours on offer – and why, oh why, would you limit yourself to just one thing anyway!

This is our collective story and journey. It brings us to this moment and we shape its next chapter with our choices. How we live. What we stand and fight for. How we love, and how deeply and intentionally we do it.

Τουρσί

Toursi | Pickled vegetables

MEZZE DISH

1 teaspoon salt

4 garlic cloves

¼ red capsicum (bell pepper), deseeded and thickly sliced

¼ yellow capsicum (bell pepper), deseeded and thickly sliced

2 bay leaves

6 florets cauliflower

2 carrots, thickly sliced

white vinegar (enough to fill half of the pickling jar you are using)

canola oil, to cover the top of the jar if refrigerating

extra-virgin olive oil, to cover the top of the jar if not refrigerating

Toursi is the Greek word for pickled vegetables. There are literally dozens of variations to this recipe. You can pick any vegetables that you like – carrots, celery, capsicums (bell peppers), fennel, zucchinis (courgettes), green tomatoes to name a few. Every region of Greece loves to pickle and has its own unique way of making and flavouring them, from wild sea fennel in Karpathos to capers pickled in Santorini.

Toursi is a popular mezze for Greeks during their 40 days of fasting before Easter and one you will find on the table of every taverna you dine at in Greece. We love to preserve vegetables to get us through the cold winter months.

You will need a sterilised pickling jar that seals well with a lid (I have used one with a capacity of about 1 litre/34 fl oz but you can use any size you like).

Add salt, garlic, vegetables and bay leaves to the jar, alternating and layering different vegetables to make the jar look as colourful as possible. Once you have reached the top, fill half the jar with very hot water and the other half with white vinegar, leaving enough room to top it up with a few tablespoons of extra-virgin olive oil if not refrigerating. If refrigerating, use canola oil, as olive oil will freeze and thicken in the fridge.

Place the lid on your jar and close tightly. Leave it to sit for at least 2 weeks to get a fuller flavour out of the vegetables. Toursi left unopened can keep for months, if not longer. Once opened, it can be refrigerated for months.

MAKE IT VEGAN

It already is!

MAKE IT GLUTEN-FREE

It already is!

WHAT TO DO WITH LEFTOVERS

Toursi can safely last for 6 months in the refrigerator. Once opened, refrigerate and top up with a little canola oil.

Σουτζουκάκια

Soutzoukakia | Vegetarian rice croquettes

SERVES 4

SOUTZOUKAKIA MIX
875 ml (29½ fl oz/3½ cups)
    water
1 teaspoon salt
300 g (10½ oz/1½ cups)
    medium-grain rice
1 teaspoon dried parsley
1 teaspoon dried mint
1 teaspoon dried basil
1 onion, finely grated
100 g (3½ oz/1 cup)
    kefalograviera, coarsely
    grated
½ teaspoon sweet paprika
2 tablespoons plain
    (all purpose) flour, plus
    extra for dusting
2 eggs, beaten
2 tablespoons extra-virgin
    olive oil
salt and pepper, to taste
canola oil, for frying

DIPPING SAUCE
250 g (9 oz/1 cup) Greek-style
    yoghurt
1 tablespoon honey
finely chopped mint, to garnish

Soutzoukakia are usually made with ground beef, but here is my vegetarian version. I've replaced the beef with medium-grain rice, and kefalograviera with a Greek-style yoghurt dipping sauce. Another option is to finish them with a rich tomato sauce (just use any of the tomato sauce recipes in this book) and grated mizithra.

Combine water and salt in a large saucepan and bring to the boil.

Add rice and cook for about 20 minutes, or until rice is cooked and all the water has evaporated. Set aside to cool to room temperature.

Once cool, place the rice in a bowl and add the dried herbs, onion, kefalograviera, paprika, flour, eggs, olive oil and salt and pepper to season.

Mix together to form a thick mixture, then cover the bowl with plastic wrap and refrigerate for an hour.

Heat canola oil in a frying pan until hot. Scoop a little of the mix into your hand and shape as pictured. You can shape it into any shape you like, it will be equally delicious. Gently roll in a plate of plain flour and shake off excess flour and then fry for about 5 minutes on each side, or until golden.

A tip here, when cooking with something patted in flour, you will find the oil gets dirty, so it's best to change the oil halfway through cooking your batch.

To make the dipping sauce, combine Greek-style yoghurt, honey and mint in a small bowl. Serve with the soutzoukakia.

MAKE IT VEGAN
Replace the eggs with a vegan egg mix and use vegan hard cheeses such as vegan cheddar and parmesan.

MAKE IT GLUTEN-FREE
Use gluten-free flour and breadcrumbs.

WHAT TO DO WITH LEFTOVERS
Make into little round fried vegan meatballs to add with your thick tomato sauce for your favourite pasta.

Κολοκυθοκεφτέδες με σιμιγδάλι και πολέντα

Semolina and polenta zucchini fritters

MEZZE DISH

2 large zucchinis (courgettes), trimmed and sliced into 3–5mm (⅛ in–¼ in) slices
salt and pepper, to taste
2 eggs
150 g (5½ oz/1 cup) plain (all-purpose) flour
125 g (4½ oz/1 cup) semolina
150 g (5½ oz/1 cup) polenta
250 ml (8½ fl oz/1 cup) cold water
250 ml (8½ fl oz/1 cup) canola oil
250 g (9 oz/1 cup) Greek-style yoghurt
1 lemon, cut into wedges

Zucchinis (courgettes) are so versatile – they are wonderful in a salad, perfect stuffed as yemista with a herbed rice mixture, or fried lathera-style in tomato and olive oil. I love to create divine pizzas with them and they are one of the stars of the classic vegan casserole dish, briam.

Place zucchini slices on a platter, season with salt and pepper and set aside for 30 minutes.

Set up your workstation: you will need three plates and two small bowls.

In a small bowl, beat the eggs. Place the flour, semolina and polenta on a separate plate each. Place water in a separate small bowl.

Heat oil in a large frying pan over a medium heat until hot.

Dip the zucchini slices first in the eggs, then in the flour, then in the polenta, next the semolina and then quickly in and out of the water. If you want a smoother texture, hold the zucchini in between your two hands and smooth them with your palms before frying to pat down further.

Add zucchini to the pan and cook, in batches, for 2–3 minutes each side, turning and cooking, until golden. Transfer to a plate lined with a paper towel to soak up excess oil. Serve with Greek-style yoghurt and lemon wedges to squeeze over to bring out their full flavours.

MAKE IT VEGAN
It already is!

MAKE IT GLUTEN-FREE
By using gluten-free flour and semolina.

WHAT TO DO WITH LEFTOVERS
Make a simple Greek tomato sauce and pour it over the fried zucchini (courgette). Crumble over some feta or grate over some mizithra.

Μαραθοκεφτέδες

Marathokeftedes | Fennel fritters

SERVES 4

375 ml (12½ fl oz/1½ cups) lager beer

60 g (2 oz/1 cup) dill, chopped, plus extra, to serve

135 g (5 oz/1 cup) finely diced leek

155 g (5½ oz/1 cup) grated carrot

1 onion, finely diced

3 spring onions (scallions), finely chopped

300 g (10½ oz/2 cups) plain (all-purpose) flour

2 eggs

3 tablespoons extra-virgin olive oil

salt and pepper, to taste

500 ml (17 fl oz/2 cups) canola oil, for frying

100 g (3½ oz) Greek-style yoghurt

The fresh dill in these fritters provides a beautiful, intense, unexpected flavour. In Ancient Greece, dill (anithos) was used to flavour wine, both for its medicinal purposes and to use in cooking. It is thought that Hippocrates himself, the father of medicine, used dill to heal wounds and aid digestion. Today Greeks use it for everything from our beloved tzatziki to flavouring soups, salads and sauces. Dill, along with Greek oregano, basil, parsley and mint, all have their own Greek variants which taste different and better than the common varieties.

Combine all ingredients except canola oil and yoghurt in a large bowl to form a thick batter.

Heat 4 tablespoons of the canola oil in a large frying pan over a medium heat. Add large tablespoonfuls of the batter, in batches, and cook for 5 minutes on each side, or until golden brown. Add more canola oil as you go, as needed. Top with Greek-style yoghurt and extra dill to serve.

MAKE IT VEGAN

Replace the eggs with a vegan egg mix or leave out altogether. Use a Greek-style soy, plant-based or coconut yoghurt.

MAKE IT GLUTEN-FREE

Use gluten-free flour and gluten-free beer

WHAT TO DO WITH LEFTOVERS

Freeze the mix and defrost the night before using. Roll into small patties, patting in a plate of plain flour on each side before frying.

Ντοματοκεφτέδες

Domatokeftedes | Tomato fritters

MEZZE DISH

6 tomatoes, finely diced
¾ teaspoon salt
1 red onion, finely diced
2 spring onions (scallions),
    finely chopped
150 g (5½ oz/1 cup) self-
    raising (self-rising) flour
1 teaspoon baking powder
1 teaspoon finely chopped
    lemon thyme
1 tablespoon finely chopped
    dill
20 g (¾ oz/⅓ cup) fresh mint,
    finely chopped
1 tablespoon finely chopped
    basil
2 tablespoons finely chopped
    flat-leaf (Italian) parsley
2 teaspoons Greek oregano
50 g (1¾ oz/½ cup)
    kefalograviera, grated
50 g (1¾ oz) halloumi, grated
1 egg
salt and pepper, to taste
250 ml (8½ fl oz/1 cup)
    canola oil

Who hasn't dreamt of spending their summertime on the Greek island of Santorini with some of the world's most stunning beaches, waking up staring at the Aegean waters and breathtaking whitewashed churches and houses, and then walking down to a local sun-soaked tavern to enjoy fresh food lovingly made by locals? These Santorini tomato keftedes are a favourite there, and for good reason – they go down so easily on a summer night with a chilled riesling wine or an ice-cold beer. When cooking, try not to use tomatoes that are too ripe, as tomatoes that are too juicy will be difficult to bind into keftedes.

Put chopped tomato in colander, cover in salt and set aside for 30 minutes to drain.

Combine drained tomatoes, the onion and spring onions, flour, baking powder, herbs, cheese, egg, salt and pepper. Set aside for 1 hour in the fridge to help the mixture bind.

Heat half the canola oil in a large frying pan and fry the keftedes, in 2 batches, and using new oil each time, until they are golden brown on both sides. Transfer to a plate lined with a paper towel to absorb excess oil. Plate and serve.

MAKE IT VEGAN

Use a vegan egg mix and vegan kefalograviera and halloumi.

MAKE IT GLUTEN-FREE

Use gluten-free flour.

WHAT TO DO WITH LEFTOVERS

You can freeze any uncooked leftovers in a zip-lock bag for up to 3 months. Defrost before cooking.

Κολοκυθοκεφτέδες

Kolokithokeftedes | Pumpkin fritters

SERVES 4

500 g (1 lb 2 oz) butternut
    pumpkin (squash), grated
2 tablespoons extra-virgin
    olive
1 onion, finely diced
1 teaspoon sweet paprika
3 eggs
3 tablespoons breadcrumbs
110 g (4 oz) plain
    (all-purpose) flour
2 tablespoons chopped dill
2 tablespoons chopped mint
3 spring onions (scallions),
    chopped
1 teaspoon salt, plus extra
    to season
50 g (1¾ oz) Greek feta or
    kefalograviera, grated
200 ml (7 fl oz) canola oil

These are beyond scrumptious and, to be honest, you really cannot eat just one: more like 12 at a time! They are so soft, the sweet pumpkin (squash) contrasting beautifully with the fresh herbs, garlic, sweet paprika and eggs. You can grate any other Greek cheeses you like, such as manouri or halloumi, into the mix too to give it an extra cheesy gooeyness.

Place pumpkin in a bowl, season with salt and set aside for 15 minutes. Squeeze the pumpkin a little with your hands to get the excess juices out (do not wash the salt off).

Combine grated pumpkin, oil, onion, paprika, eggs, breadcrumbs, 1 tablespoon of the flour, herbs, spring onion, salt and cheese in a large bowl, mixing with a wooden spoon to form a thick mixture.

Place remaining flour on a plate.

Heat canola oil in a large frying pan over a medium heat. Shape tablespoonfuls of the mixture into small patties, dip in a little flour and fry for 2–3 minutes on each side, or until golden (add small amounts of canola oil as needed as the patties absorb it – remember you are frying, not deep-frying, them). Transfer cooked patties to a plate lined with a paper towel to drain excess oil, then serve.

MAKE IT VEGAN

Replace the eggs with a vegan egg mix or leave out altogether. Use a Greek-style soy, plant-based or coconut yoghurt.

MAKE IT GLUTEN-FREE

Use gluten-free flour.

WHAT TO DO WITH LEFTOVERS

Use as a filling for sweet fried or baked phyllo pastries.

Σκορδαλιά

Skordalia | Garlic potato dip

SERVES 4

6 potatoes, peeled and
    quartered
125 ml (4 fl oz/½ cup)
    extra-virgin olive oil,
    plus extra to serve
6 garlic cloves, minced
2 teaspoons white-wine
    vinegar
salt and pepper, to taste
½ spring onion (scallion),
    finely chopped, to garnish
60 g (2 oz/1 cup) flat-leaf
    (Italian) parsley, chopped

This dish is not recommended if you plan to have a pash afterwards, as you will be carrying the strong scent of garlic all over you, but otherwise it's delicious. I like to make it the traditional way with a mortar and pestle. How skordalia is made varies across regions of Greece – for example, in Crete or the Ionian Islands, we add walnuts or almonds, or soaked bread, to the mashed potatoes. I like to stir the spring onions (scallions) and parsley through the potatoes at the end to give it more colour, or you can just have on top as a garnish.

Add potatoes to a large pot of water, bring to the boil, then reduce heat to a gentle simmer and cook for 30 minutes, or until tender without going to mush. Drain and set aside for 5 minutes.

In a mortar, combine olive oil, garlic, white-wine vinegar and season with salt. Pound with a pestle until well combined, then transfer to a small bowl and set aside.

Place potatoes either one at a time into the mortar and mash or place all in a bowl and mash. Using a fork, stir in garlic mixture until combined and season to taste. Sprinkle with spring onion and parsley, and drizzle with more oil to serve.

MAKE IT VEGAN
It already is!

MAKE IT GLUTEN-FREE
It already is!

WHAT TO DO WITH LEFTOVERS
This delicious dip keeps well
refrigerated for up to a week.

Μεσσηνιακές Πλακοτηγανίτες

Messinian plakotiganites | Greek crêpes with mizithra

SERVES 4

300 g (10½ oz/2 cups) plain (all-purpose) flour
1 teaspoon salt
560 ml (19 fl oz/2¼ cups) water
80 ml (2½ fl oz/⅓ cup) extra-virgin olive oil
35 g (1¼ oz/⅓ cup) grated mizithra

This heavenly crêpe with salty mizithra cheese is unique to the region of Messinia, where my mum, Sia, was born and grew up. My mum's hometown, Messina, on the slopes of Mount Ithomi, was the region's ancient capital. The modern capital, Kalamata, is Messinia's largest city, home to Kalamata olives and the olive oil that Homer called liquid gold. Blessed with some of Greece's most beautiful mountain ranges and beaches, Messinia's fertile lands are truly sunkissed. You'll find olive groves, vineyards and blossoming fig trees as far as the eye can see.

Mix all ingredients, except mizithra, in a bowl to combine. You don't want the mixture to be dry and thick, but rather wet and the consistency of a béchamel sauce.

It's vital to use a non-stick pan for this recipe as, at first, we don't use any oil to fry these little Greek crêpes.

Heat a non-stick frying pan over a medium heat until hot. Pour in about half a soup ladle of the mixture, as if you are making a thin pancake. Swoosh the pan around so that the batter moves across the pan and does not clump. Cook for about 2 minutes and then flip over to cook on the other side for 2 minutes, or until both sides have a nice light brown colour. Now stack each one on top of the other and repeat with remaining batter.

Heat the olive oil in the same small pan until it is very hot.

Now we want to fry just one side of each crêpe. So you are going to take each one and slowly drag one side through the hot olive oil, leaving it in the pan for 8–10 seconds and then placing on a plate. Do this to one side of each crêpe and place on top of each other as you go. Be careful as you go, and watch the oil to avoid burning your hands with the oil.

Roll each crêpe into a cigar and sprinkle with mizithra to serve.

MAKE IT VEGAN

By using a vegan hard cheese.

MAKE IT GLUTEN-FREE

By using a gluten-free flour.

WHAT TO DO WITH LEFTOVERS

You could fill the leftover crêpes with fruits and cover them with Greek-style yoghurt and cinnamon for a delicious breakfast dish.

Τηγανητά πατατάκια

My halloumi, olive and eggplant baked eggs

SERVES 2

180 g (2½ fl oz/about
    1½ cups) finely diced
    eggplant (aubergine)
salt, to season
80 ml (2½ fl oz/⅓ cup)
    extra-virgin olive oil
1 red onion, finely diced
1 teaspoon sugar
2 garlic cloves, finely chopped
2 spring onions (scallions),
    roughly chopped
200 g (2½ fl oz) drained and
    rinsed tinned butter beans
4 tomatoes, freshly diced
1 tablespoon tomato paste
1 teaspoon sweet paprika
125 ml (4 fl oz/½ cup) water
1 teaspoon finely chopped
    mint
salt and pepper, to taste
8 large green olives, halved
4 eggs
250 g (2½ fl oz) halloumi,
    thickly sliced
1 teaspoon sumac or za'atar

This is a Greek twist on the traditional North African
and Middle Eastern dish shakshuka, which I absolutely
adore. Remember it is really important to salt the eggplant
(aubergine) before you cook, to get the bitterness out. You can
also leave out the butter beans or use cannellini, black beans or
chickpeas, which also work well. You can finish this dish with
a garnish of freshly chopped mint, parsley, Greek oregano or
basil. Instead of eggplant, you can bake these eggs with roasted
pumpkin (winter squash), sweet potato, zucchinis (courgettes)
and use grated kasseri, kefalograviera or graviera.

Place eggplant in a bowl, season with salt, cover with water and
set aside for 30 minutes. Drain and pat dry on paper towels.

To make the sauce, heat olive oil in a frying pan over a low heat.
Sauté onion and sugar for 2 minutes, or until softened. Add
garlic and spring onion and cook for a further 2 minutes. Add
eggplant and continue to cook for 5 minutes. Add beans,
tomatoes, tomato paste, sweet paprika, water and mint and
season with salt and pepper. Cook for a further 15 minutes,
or until the sauce thickens.

Preheat the oven to 200°C (390°F).

Spoon some of the sauce into the base of a baking dish. Scatter
olives in the dish then, using a spoon, create 4 little pockets in the
sauce. Break an egg into each of the 4 pockets. Top with halloumi
slices and sumac, cover with foil and bake for 15 minutes. Remove
foil and bake for a further 10–15 minutes, or until eggs are
well baked.

MAKE IT VEGAN

By using vegan halloumi and
replacing the eggs with a vegan egg
mix or leave out altogether.

MAKE IT GLUTEN-FREE

It already is!

WHAT TO DO WITH LEFTOVERS

They make a fantastic pita bread
filling for lunch with some salad.

Ομελέτα με ασημένια τεύτλα, σπανάκι και φέτα

Silverbeet, spinach and feta omelette

SERVES 2

125 g (4½ oz) silverbeet (Swiss chard), roughly chopped
125 g (4½ oz) English spinach, roughly chopped
80 ml (2½ fl oz/⅓ cup) extra-virgin olive oil
salt and pepper, to taste, plus extra for serving
3 eggs
100 g (3½ oz) Greek feta

My garden has been overflowing with silverbeet (Swiss chard) all year and I have been trying to find as many creative ways as I can to use it. One of the delightful surprises has been how incredible it is as part of an omelette. Although, you can use any greens such as rocket (arugula), spinach leaves, rapini or endives just as well. Likewise, any cheese is wonderful as part of this, such as kaseri, kefalograviera, manouri or graviera.

Make sure to thoroughly wash the silverbeet and spinach before using. A good way to do this is to soak them both in a bowl of water first to make sure all the dirt is removed. Cut off the roots of the spinach if you have bought it as a bunch and not just as leaves.

Heat 2 tablespoons of the extra-virgin olive oil in a frying pan over a low heat, and sauté the silverbeet and spinach until wilted (what looks like too much to fit into a pan will wilt significantly down to make a delicious filling for the omelette). Drizzle the remaining olive oil over the spinach and silverbeet as it wilts to help the process. Season with salt and pepper.

Meanwhile, beat eggs and feta together in a large bowl.

Once the greens have wilted, pour evenly over the egg mixture, making sure to keep swirling the pan to get the mix all over, and cook for 2 minutes. If the egg mix is too much for the pan, gently use a fork to make small holes in the omelette so the egg mix can spread.

Take a plate big enough to cover the pan and place it on top of your frying pan. Hold the handle of your pan and quickly flip the omelette over and then slide it back onto the pan and you suddenly get a beautiful cooked omelette on both sides, with all the vibrant green colours on show. Cook for another minute and then slide onto a serving plate and finish with some salt and pepper to taste.

MAKE IT VEGAN

Replace the eggs with a vegan egg mix and a vegan Greek feta.

MAKE IT GLUTEN-FREE

It already is!

WHAT TO DO WITH LEFTOVERS

Makes a wonderful filling for sandwiches the next day.

φρουτάλια

Froutalia | Greek omelette

SERVES 4

2 potatoes, peeled and
    thinly sliced about 3 mm
    (⅛ in) thick
1 tablespoon dried Greek
    oregano
salt and pepper, to taste
canola oil, for frying
3 eggs, beaten
1 teaspoon finely chopped
    rosemary
1 teaspoon fresh thyme
1 teaspoon chopped flat-leaf
    (Italian) parsley
1 teaspoon chopped mint
50 g (1¾ oz) Kalamata olives,
    pitted and sliced
50 g (1¾ oz) Greek feta,
    crumbled

Traditionally made with potatoes and sausages, froutalia is
a moreish omelette that originates from the Cyclades islands.
This is my vegetarian version. I love the golden brown of the
fried potatoes, and with the eggs and feta, it's almost like a
Greek fries omelette! You can also substitute the potatoes
for a range of different vegetables such as sliced zucchini
(courgette), eggplant (aubergine), pumpkin (winter squash)
or artichokes.

Toss potato slices with Greek oregano and season with salt and
pepper to taste.

Heat 2–3 tablespoons of oil in a frying pan until hot. Add potato
and fry on both sides until golden (keep a close eye on them to
make sure they don't burn). Once cooked, transfer to a plate
lined with a paper towel to drain excess oil.

Let your pan cool down for a few minutes and wipe clean with
a paper towel. Add fresh canola oil.

Combine eggs, herbs, olives and feta in a large bowl.

Return the pan over a medium heat and cover the base with slices
of cooked potato. Pour over the egg mixture, using a fork to prick
little holes into the potatoes, and cook for 2 minutes.

Place a plate that covers the whole pan on top of the pan to cover
it and quickly and carefully flip the pan over so the omelette is on
the plate. Slide it back into the pan to cook for a further 2 minutes
so both sides are evenly cooked.

MAKE IT VEGAN

Replace the eggs with a vegan egg mix
and use vegan feta.

MAKE IT GLUTEN-FREE

It already is!

WHAT TO DO WITH LEFTOVERS

Even cold this dish is great and could
easily be sliced up as an afternoon
mezze snack or as part of dinner.

FAMILY

In my family there is no mine and yours, nothing is transactional. For all the stressors that can come with the heaviness of family expectation at times, it is a love so enduring, so powerful and precious that I would never forsake it.

My mother, Sia, loves so fiercely, and no more than through her cooking. It is her gift to her children that has triumphed over the poverty, racism and hardship she endured with my father, Leo. My mum's love for her family is a love that can never be dimmed or defeated. There is nothing like food made by someone who loves you unconditionally. It is food that tastes like home.

Food, in my family, was an ever present act of love, a constant. I think of my mum making spanakopita with a hand-made phyllo pastry after a long week at the factory. My dad making sure to bring me a chocolate bar every day after work, no matter how late the hour was. Me as an eight-year-old cooking an extravagant feast of baked beans, eggs and sausages after school for my sister, Nola, and myself as our parents worked late on the tobacco farms.

Food was the way my mum would show her love for me and my sister growing up. To this day, she cooks the most elaborate and lovingly made meals. My sister, Nola, carries on that tradition in creating nutritious, beautifully homemade meals for her two children, Leo and Sia. This work, so often dismissed as 'women's work', devalued and taken for granted, is the hard work that kept my family together and gave my sister and me the choices my mum never had.

Wine and children speak the truth.
— GREEK PROVERB

Cooking was how I connected to my culture and to my mum. It was a common language we spoke, a way for Mum and me to get close. It was the connective tissue that bridged the gap between the love felt and the love unspoken between us. We became close through Mum's sharing and her recipes and through her teaching me our culture, our roots and, most importantly, to be proud of who I am and where I came from.

Many of the memories I have of my late father, Leo, are of him in the kitchen making the greatest Greek salad I have ever tasted to this day. I can still smell and taste it. There he stood after a hard day toiling in a dyed-wool factory in his Blundstone boots, worn blue jeans rolled up and his red shirt with enough buttons open for him to proudly show off his hairy chest.

He would cut the ripest red tomatoes from his lovingly grown garden and fill the deepest bowl he could find with the thickest slices of feta to crumble over the salad. In went Greek oregano and plentiful amounts of olive oil, and then, with his powerful and weathered hands, he would toss them all together. Childhood memories of olive oil–soaked bread and of the pride my father had on his face when he could see the joy it brought us is something I will never forget.

He would also beam like a peacock when making fasolatha and fakes. These beautiful soups bubbled on a low simmer for many hours, put together with such care and thoughtfulness. They were the warm hugs Dad did not know how to give any other way.

All of this happened with a backstory of incredible hardship and sacrifice before my parents even made it to Australia. Living off the land, having to survive off the land, harvesting crops, growing their own food – these were the themes of my parents' childhoods and adolescence. It defined them both so deeply.

My father's dreams of being the lawyer I became were lost to the realities of the poverty and hardship in which he was raised. At the tender age of nine he had to drop out of school to plough and harvest the fields and tend the farm animals with his father, something he had started at age five. Being from a poor farming family in Messina, my mum fared little better, not getting to see the inside of a school beyond the age of 12.

My maternal grandmother, Olga, had come from a wealthy family, her father being the richest man in town, and Olga had completed high school. She was destined for university and her parents had ambitions that she would become a doctor. My grandfather Paul met Olga while working as a farm hand on her parents' farm. Paul and Olga fell in love and eloped. Her father disowned her and for love she gave up her wealth and they began together with nothing but each other. When her father died she was left out of his will.

Raising their children off the land as farmers, my grandparents were grateful to be able to cook with whatever they could grow, barter for or forage.

They were potato farmers living in a home they built with their own hands. Twice a year they would harvest their potatoes, and they eventually found themselves in the food markets of Athens selling their produce, including nuts. They would also make their own olive oil from a small olive grove at their home. As a little girl, my mum would knock the olives down with sticks, for gathering each autumn. They would then fill hessian sacks with olives to be taken for making into olive oil in Kalamata.

My yiayia Olga and grandfather Paul would make little miracles from what Olga could grow too, be it eggplants (aubergines), beans, tomatoes, zucchinis (courgettes) or okra. My mum recalls chickens running around providing the eggs, and a pig that would be sacrificed each year for Easter. Each Sunday they would have a roast with potatoes, and once a week my grandfather would go to the fish market to bring back fish as a treat. It was never the ingredients that made the dish, but the intention and love with which it was made.

My mum remembers eating the wild artichokes fresh from the fields, fresh petals of heaven with a crunch, with her mother's bread from a homemade wood oven to accompany them. Two fig trees and two walnut trees also offered their bounteous produce. She would wake early in the morning before the summer heat and climb one of the fig trees while the figs were still wet and cool and, together with her siblings, devour every fresh one until nothing ripe was left, and enjoy the prickled sweet joy of fragosika (prickly pear) too. She recalls the pomegranate trees in the heart of summer, and breaking open the fruit with her hands, then plunging face first into them. She recalls, too, the sweet summer joy signalled by the lemon and apricot trees.

My mum had a trick to secure her watermelon bounty each year without her father knowing. She would carve a little hole in a watermelon to see if it was ripe. If she saw white instead of ripe red, she would gently place the cutout piece back in and turn it over in the dirt so her father would not realise what she had done.

On Greek summer mornings before the heat had taken hold of the day, they would drop the watermelon in the well to cool it and pull it out that night, as it would rise up and not sink.

Everything was fresh and from the land. My yiayia would make her own feta, her own pasta – trahana and hilopites in winter – and mizithra cheese. A lamb would provide the daily milk. My grandmother even made her own soap from the pig fat. Nothing went to waste –my grandmother would use the clothes from her dowry and cut them up to make clothes for her kids. I come from a generation of strong, indefatigable women. My great grandmother Georgia lived to the age of 104 and she still cooked and washed until her last year.

The fields of my grandparents' farms would be ploughed by Koula, my mum's childhood horse. Every day after ploughing the fields to grow the food her family would sell and live off, my mum would brush Koula's coat. They used to go up and down the village streets bareback. The baby lambs that would be reared each year and sacrificed at Easter, would be my mum's childhood friends in between. She used to make the lambs run back and forth to do exercise, and would weep when Easter came around and the lambs met their sad fate.

For my yiayia Parthena, a meal was an act of love too. As it was for my mum, it was also an act of sacrifice, and if there wasn't enough to go around, they made sure their children ate before them. Most importantly, meals were the time when family came together.

My grandparents Parthena and Konstantinos were tobacco farmers in the small town of Apsilo. They were both refugees from the region of Pontus, having been uprooted from their ancestors' homeland of nearly 3000 years at the hands of Turkey, which committed genocide, killing more than a million Greeks, 353,000 from Pontus alone. The Pontian people are a group indigenous to the region of Pontus, on the shores of the Black Sea and in the Pontic Mountains of Northeastern Anatolia (now colonised and known as Turkey).

The food culture and history of Pontus followed the seasons, due to the harshness of the mountainous region. The unpredictability of the seasons and brutal winters forced its people to find ways to stockpile and preserve foods for the months in which nothing would grow – from pickling vegetables, salting fish and drying fruits and vegetables to preparing pre-cooked pastas and cheeses that were made from the summer dairy bounties.

My grandparents' village had a brutal and cold climate, with snow engulfing it in the winter months. Tobacco farming was a harsh job; the tobacco would be painstakingly dried in the sun each summer. My dad, Leo, had to work the tobacco farms to help his father raise a dowry so his three sisters could be married. Every dollar he made, my dad would give to his mother. He would stand outside the sweet shops and savour the smells but never allow himself to have anything.

Almost anything they could grow my grandad would strap to the donkey and walk to Edessa markets to sell and barter as best as he could.

These struggles to survive, to provide for their families, grounds me and provides perspective, giving me pride in where I have come from and gratitude for the choices I now have.

Στραπατσάδα

Strapatsada | Eggs and zucchini

SERVES 2

80 ml (2½ fl oz/⅓ cup)
　　extra-virgin olive oil
3 zucchinis (courgettes), diced
6 eggs, beaten
salt and pepper, to taste
1 teaspoon Greek oregano
100 g (3½ oz) Greek feta

This is a dish enjoyed at breakfast or lunch or as a snack in Greece. It is incredibly popular because of the ease and speed with which it can be made (it is particularly popular on the Ionian Islands). It is a dish that originated from the Peloponnese and it is the perfect go-to for breakfast, as you can have it ready in 20 minutes. You can use eggplant (aubergine) instead of zucchini (courgette), if you like.

Heat olive oil in a medium frying pan over a medium heat, add zucchini and cook for about 10 minutes, or until softened. Pour in eggs and shake the pan to distribute them evenly. Season with salt and pepper, stir gently and cook for a further 5 minutes or so until the egg is just set. Sprinkle with Greek oregano and feta to serve.

MAKE IT VEGAN

Replace the eggs with a vegan egg mix, and use vegan Greek feta.

MAKE IT GLUTEN-FREE

It already is!

WHAT TO DO WITH LEFTOVERS

A heavenly filling for pita breads with salad or enjoyed cold as a snack later that night.

Καγιανάς

Kagianas | Eggs and tomato

SERVES 2

4 tomatoes, peeled and
    finely chopped
80 ml (2½ fl oz/⅓ cup)
    extra-virgin olive oil
½ red onion, finely chopped
2 spring onions (scallions)
6 eggs, beaten
1 teaspoon Greek oregano
100 g (3½ oz) Greek feta
1 tablespoon of salt
salt and pepper to taste

In Greek cooking, strapatsada and kagianas are part of the same family of scrambled egg goodness. This is just a variation on the same theme, but instead of zucchini (courgette) being the hero of the dish, it is juicy red tomatoes that get the spotlight. Both these dishes came to popularity in Greece because they were the dish of the poor in Arcadia, where they could take what they had in their own yards – from their chickens to their vegetables – and create a filling, nutritious meal.

For this dish, it is really important to peel the tomato skins off, as the real flavour lies underneath, and you do not want to leave the tomato peels swimming around. Fresh tomatoes really are much better, but if you cannot afford them or access them, tinned diced tomatoes will do just fine instead. I love eating this dish straight out of the pan with crusty bread.

Heat a large saucepan of water over a medium heat and bring to the boil. Make a little cross with a sharp knife at the bottom of each tomato (just a shallow cut, not a deep one) and add to the boiling water. Blanch for 2 minutes, then set aside to cool. Once cool enough to handle, peel off the skin and dice the flesh into cubes.

As tomatoes have so many juices, it is a good idea to then place them in a colander and sprinkle with 1 tablespoon of salt. Set aside for 10–15 minutes to drain excess water from the tomatoes. Without doing this you run the risk of a watery omelette or one that will take much longer to cook.

Heat the olive oil in a medium frying pan over a low heat.

Add onions and tomatoes and cook for about 10 minutes, or until the cooking liquid has reduced. Pour in eggs and shake the pan gently to distribute the eggs evenly. Continue to cook for 3–5 minutes until the egg has cooked through. Season with salt and pepper and sprinkle with Greek oregano and feta to serve.

MAKE IT VEGAN

Replace the eggs with a vegan egg mix and vegan Greek feta.

MAKE IT GLUTEN-FREE

It already is!

WHAT TO DO WITH LEFTOVERS

Enjoy with some rice, on toast the next day for breakfast, add some beans and re-fry up or add to your sandwiches, wraps or burgers.

Τυροκαυτερή

Tirokafteri | Feta and yoghurt dip

MEZZE DISH

200 g (7 oz) Greek-style
  yoghurt
¼ teaspoon salt
2 red capsicums
  (bell peppers)
80 ml (2½ fl oz/⅓ cup)
  extra-virgin olive oil, plus
  extra for drizzling
3 garlic cloves
½ teaspoon cayenne pepper
½ teaspoon chilli flakes
200 g (7 oz) Greek feta,
  crumbled
salt and pepper, to taste
15 g (½ oz/½ cup) chopped
  Italian (flat-leaf) parsley
10 g (½ oz/½ cup) chopped
  mint
bread, to serve

This is a dip that doesn't care about winning you over with its looks; it hits you where it matters, your tummy. This is a spicy, rich and creamy dip that will make the perfect addition to your mezze platter. While I think the Greek feta offers a lovely salty contrast to the capsicums (bell peppers) you can also substitute it with other Greek cheeses including manouri, mizithra or anthotyro. You can also choose to make the dip more runny and less thick by adding some more Greek yoghurt.

Place the Greek-style yoghurt in the centre of a clean tea towel or muslin cloth and sprinkle with salt. Fold up the edges of the cloth and secure with a rubber band. Hang off a sink tap in a cool place overnight to drain into the sink.

Preheat the oven to 180°C (360°F). Place capsicums in a large roasting tin and drizzle with 2 tablespoons of the oil. Roast for 30 minutes, or until they darken. Set aside to cool, then deseed and slice.

Combine sliced capsicum, garlic, remaining oil, cayenne pepper and chilli flakes in a blender and process until smooth.

Transfer mixture to a bowl and stir in the feta and drained yoghurt. Season to taste and sprinkle with parsley and mint. Drizzle with olive oil and serve with your favourite bread.

MAKE IT VEGAN

By using a Greek-style soy, plant-based or coconut yoghurt and a vegan Greek feta.

MAKE IT GLUTEN-FREE

It already is!

WHAT TO DO WITH LEFTOVERS

Use the leftover dip as a spread over toast with eggs for breakfast or use as a filling for a vegetarian or vegan Greek pita wrap with tomato, cucumbers and feta.

Ντιπ φάβας

Fava dip

MEZZE DISH

500 g (1 lb 2 oz) yellow split
  peas
80 ml (2½ fl oz/⅓ cup)
  extra-virgin olive oil
1½ onions, finely diced
1½ litres (51 fl oz/6 cups)
  water
salt and pepper, to taste
1 teaspoon Greek oregano
  or thyme
juice of 1 lemon or 1 tablespoon
  of white vinegar

This flavourful, creamy and smooth dip, made from yellow split peas, is one of the most traditional dips in Greek food culture. Its beauty is in the simplicity of its ingredients and it would have to be the most affordable dip you could make. I love to enjoy it cold, served with finely diced onion on top, along with dried Greek oregano and extra-virgin olive oil. It is best served with bread, olives, feta and wine on the side.

Place split peas in a large bowl, cover with boiling water, stir for 1 minute, then drain in a colander.

Heat olive oil in a large frying pan and fry two-thirds of the diced onion for 4–5 minutes, or until golden. Add the split peas and fry for a further 2 minutes and then add all the water.

Bring to the boil then reduce to simmer over a low heat and cook for about 1 hour, until all the juices are absorbed and you have a thick, creamy soup.

With 5 minutes to go, season with salt and pepper.

If you want a smooth consistency, you can use a stick blender to blend the mixture for 1 minute. Or for more texture, mash with a fork to reach desired consistency. Transfer to a serving bowl and add remaining onion, Greek oregano or thyme and either the lemon or vinegar.

MAKE IT VEGAN

It already is!

MAKE IT GLUTEN-FREE

It already is!

WHAT TO DO WITH LEFTOVERS

It is delicious cold the next day drizzled with some extra-virgin olive oil and topped with extra Greek oregano and chopped spring onions (scallions) to refresh it.

Τζατζίκι

Tzatziki | Cucumber and yoghurt dip

MEZZE DISH

1 kg (2 lb 3 oz) Greek-style yoghurt
3 Lebanese cucumbers, grated (with excess moisture squeezed out)
½ teaspoon salt
4 garlic cloves, finely diced
2 tablespoons extra-virgin olive oil, plus extra to serve
4 tablespoons white vinegar
handful of dill, chopped, and extra to sprinkle on top and serve

Once you've made tzatziki at home, you'll never want to eat store-bought again. The flavour, colour and texture is unparalleled. It is the perfect dip to have as part of any mezze. Greeks have adored this dish since ancient times, when it was called mittiko. It is a side dish that accompanies every shared Greek meal, along with pita bread and a Greek salad. While dill is what gives tzatziki its incredible flavour and colour, in some regions of Greece, fresh Greek oregano, mint or thyme are used. You can spread it over pita bread, dip your fritters in it, use it as a base for flatbread pizzas, as a filling for your vegan or vegetarian kebab, or spread it over your morning toast.

To drain the yoghurt in the traditional Greek way as I do, scoop the yoghurt into the centre of the thinnest (clean) tea towel you have, fold in the edges like a parcel and tie it up using a rubber band. If you have a sink in a cool place, hang the yoghurt parcel from the tap so the liquid strains through the tea towel into the sink.

An alternative method is to line a colander or strainer with a very thin tea towel or muslin cloth and place over a bowl (making sure there is plenty of space between the base of the strainer and the bowl to catch the liquid). Spoon yoghurt into the lined strainer and place in a cool place to drain overnight.

The next day, place the drained yoghurt in a large bowl. Add cucumber, salt, garlic, oil, vinegar and dill and stir to combine. Drizzle with extra oil and set aside.

MAKE IT VEGAN

By using a Greek-style soy, plant-based or coconut yoghurt.

MAKE IT GLUTEN-FREE

It already is!

WHAT TO DO WITH LEFTOVERS

This dip will safely last for at least two weeks covered in your fridge with some more olive oil drizzled on top. Perfect for wraps, salads, sandwiches and crackers every day!

Μελιτζανοσαλάτα

Melitzanosalata | Eggplant dip

MEZZE DISH

3 eggplants (aubergines)
5 g (⅛ oz/¼ cup) flat-leaf (Italian) parsley, plus extra to serve
2 garlic cloves, finely chopped
125 ml (4 fl oz/½ cup) lemon juice
3 teaspoons white vinegar
125 ml (4 fl oz/½ cup) extra-virgin olive oil, plus extra to serve
salt and pepper, to taste

I love scooping into this smoky eggplant (aubergine) dip with fresh pita bread, or spreading it over thick toasted crusty bread with a drizzle of extra-virgin olive oil and crumbled Greek feta.

When making this dish, you can puree, mash it or leave it more rustic-style, with the texture of the eggplant intact. If you want to make it creamier, you can add Greek-style yoghurt and crushed walnuts.

A tip if you want to make it extra smoky: grill the eggplants whole on your barbecue to get that full charcoal smoky flavour. I pierce the eggplants all over with a fork before doing this, as it makes it easier to grill. I prefer to mash the dip by hand rather than using a food processor, as I love a thick, chunky texture, served with an extra drizzling of olive oil and lemon juice, of course!

Place whole eggplants directly on the top of your gas hotplate. Roast over the flame for about 5 minutes, turning until charred, soft and smoky.

Set aside to cool, then peel, roughly chop the flesh and transfer to a bowl and gently mash. Add parsley, garlic, lemon juice, white vinegar, oil and season with salt and pepper to taste. Mix to combine. Drizzle with extra oil and sprinkle with parsley to serve.

MAKE IT VEGAN

It already is!

MAKE IT GLUTEN-FREE

It already is!

WHAT TO DO WITH LEFTOVERS

This dip is beautiful on toasted bread for breakfast with kasseri, manouri or kefalotyri cheese.

Ασημένια μπιφτέκια και φέτα

Silverbeet and feta patties

SERVES 4

600 g silverbeet (Swiss chard), chopped
1 egg, beaten
200 g (7 oz) Greek feta
½ teaspoon sweet paprika
1 teaspoon Greek oregano
2 tablespoons plain (all-purpose) flour
3 tablespoons breadcrumbs
30 g (1 oz/½ cup) dill, chopped
10 g (1 oz/½ cup) mint, chopped
15 g (1 oz/½ cup) flat-leaf (Italian) parsley, chopped
1 teaspoon extra-virgin olive oil
1 onion, diced
2 spring onions (scallions), diced
salt and pepper, to taste
250 ml (8½ fl oz/1 cup) canola oil
extra 150 g (5½ oz/1 cup) plain (all-purpose) flour

Silverbeet (Swiss chard) is the Greek green goddess of the garden, growing all year round, and so cheap and easy to grow. In winter, spring and summer, I've gone to my garden each day to cut these leafy temples of goodness, filled with vitamin A and K, folate and potassium, to make all my favourite dishes. From spanakorizo, spanakopita and black-eyed pea stews to dolmades and these fantastic fritters with feta, all love silverbeet.

Bring a large saucepan of salted water to the boil and cook silverbeet for 5 minutes, or until tender. Drain and set aside.

Combine egg, feta, paprika, Greek oregano, flour, breadcrumbs, herbs, olive oil, onion and spring onion in a large bowl. Add silverbeet and mix to combine. Season with salt and pepper. Refrigerate for 30 minutes to 1 hour to allow the mixture to firm.

You have two options: to dip patties in flour before cooking or opt to cook without flour. Fry without dipping into flour and you will get patties that best showcase the colours of the feta and silverbeet. If you use flour, you will get more of a golden colour.

Heat a few tablespoons of the canola oil in a large frying pan until hot. Add patties and fry, in batches, and adding more oil as it is absorbed, for 3–5 minutes on each side, or until golden.

MAKE IT VEGAN

By using vegan feta and vegan egg mix instead of eggs.

MAKE IT GLUTEN-FREE

By using gluten-free flour and breadcrumbs.

WHAT TO DO WITH LEFTOVERS

The leftover patties go great in a veggie burger or as filling for your next spanakopita (just freeze till then).

Salads

Σαλάτα με κολοκυθάκια, ρόδι και κατσικίσιο τυρί

Zucchini, pomegranate and goat's cheese salad

SERVES 4

2 large zucchinis (courgettes),
  peeled horizontally
  into strips
3 tablespoons extra-virgin
  olive oil
juice of 1 lemon
salt and pepper, to taste
seeds of ½ pomegranate
2 tablespoons roughly
  chopped mint
20 g (¾ oz) pine nuts, toasted
75 g (2¾ oz) goat's cheese

A beautiful salad for any season made in less than five minutes. Whatever your budget and however humble you make this, it's still divine. Fresh zucchini (courgette) eaten raw has incredible flavour when dressed with a little lemon, salt and olive oil. You can also use any kind of fresh herbs that you like with this dish, though mint is most complementary to the natural flavours of zucchini. If all you can afford today is the zucchini and lemon, that's still enough to make this dish sing.

Combine zucchini, oil and lemon juice in a bowl and season with salt and pepper. Massage with your hands to coat the zucchini in the oil and juice. Add pomegranate seeds, mint and pine nuts and gently combine. Crumble over goat's cheese to serve.

MAKE IT VEGAN

By using a vegan goat's cheese.

MAKE IT GLUTEN-FREE

It already is!

WHAT TO DO WITH LEFTOVERS

Toss leftovers with your favourite beans or with tomatoes, spring onions (scallions) and feta to make a delicious new salad.

Σαλάτα με αρχαία ελληνικά δημητριακά

Ancient Greek grains salad

SERVES 6

200 g (7 oz) puy lentils, rinsed

200 g (7 oz) pearl barley, rinsed

30 g (2 oz/1 cup) flat-leaf (Italian) parsley, chopped

20 g (2 oz/1 cup) mint, chopped

390 g (14 oz/2.5 cups) whole almonds, plus extra to serve

seeds of 1½ pomegranates, plus extra to serve

2 tablespoons pomegranate molasses

salt and pepper, to taste

80 ml (2½ fl oz/⅓ cup) extra-virgin olive oil, plus extra for drizzling

2 tablespoons pistachio nuts, roughly chopped

50 g (1¾ oz) Greek feta

Essential to the Greek way of life since ancient times, barley has been used not only for making wine and beer but for making porridge and flour for our bread as well. This salad is packed with so much goodness – barley is low GI and high in dietary fibre and vitamin B1, and puy lentils have one of the highest amounts of protein of any pulses. Pomegranates are rich in antioxidants and flavonoids and the almonds are rich in vitamin E and magnesium.

Bring a large pot or saucepan of water to the boil, add lentils and cook for 25–30 minutes, or until tender, then drain and rinse well.

Meanwhile, in a separate large pot or saucepan, boil barley for 25–30 minutes, or until tender, then drain and rinse well. Combine cooked lentils and barley in a bowl.

Add herbs, almonds, pomegranate seeds and pomegranate molasses and gently combine. Season to taste with salt and pepper. Drizzle with olive oil and toss to combine.

To give your salad an extra dash of beautiful colour, it is worth topping it with some more pomegranate seeds and almonds so the colours really stand out. Add pistachios and crumble feta over the salad, then drizzle with extra oil to serve.

MAKE IT VEGAN

By using a vegan feta.

MAKE IT GLUTEN-FREE

By replacing the barley with millet.

WHAT TO DO WITH LEFTOVERS

This is a salad that will easily keep for a week if refrigerated and covered. Make a whole new salad by adding spinach, rocket and Greek feta.

Ψητά ντοματίνια με κατσικίσιο τυρί

Roasted cherry tomatoes on goat's cheese

MEZZE DISH

1 kg (2 lb 3 oz) cherry
    tomatoes (multi-coloured
    or red)
2 sprigs thyme
2 sprigs rosemary
3 garlic cloves, sliced
1 teaspoon Greek oregano
80 ml (2½ fl oz/⅓ cup)
    extra-virgin olive oil
salt and pepper, to taste
250 g (9 oz) goat's cheese
30 g (1 oz/½ cup) mint, basil
    or flat-leaf (Italian) parsley,
    coarsely chopped

I love this dish so much for its simple pleasures. You can't go wrong when you place anything on goat's cheese. In this dish, I have simply roasted cherry tomatoes in a Greek marinade. You can roast these tomatoes on your barbecue, on your oven grill or even fry them in a large pan.

Preheat the oven to 180°C (360°F). Place tomatoes in a large roasting tin and toss with the thyme, rosemary, garlic, Greek oregano and olive oil. Season with salt and pepper. Cook for about 15 minutes, or until golden, soft and deeply coloured. Note as an alternative, you can also use a frying pan on low heat: add oil and garlic and fry for 1 minute, add the herbs, fry for 2 minutes, then add the tomatoes and fry for about 10 minutes, or until golden, soft and deeply coloured.

Meanwhile, spread the goat's cheese over a serving plate or small bowl.

Remove herb sprigs from the roasting tin. Top goat's cheese with roasted cherry tomatoes, drizzling over any juices from the pan. Top with remaining herbs to serve.

MAKE IT VEGAN

Use a vegan goat's cheese or other soft vegan cheese.

MAKE IT GLUTEN-FREE

It already is!

WHAT TO DO WITH LEFTOVERS

Enjoy the next morning, spread over toast or use as a pizza topping.

Σαλάτα με σύκο, κατσικίσιο τυρί, μέλι και ρόδι

Fig, goat's cheese, honey and pomegranate salad

SERVES 2

10 fresh basil leaves or
   6 sorrel leaves
2 tablespoons pomegranate
   molasses or balsamic glaze
5 fresh figs, halved
75 g (2¾ oz) goat's cheese
50 g (1¾ oz/⅓ cup) almonds
seeds from ¼ pomegranate
2 tablespoons honey

If I was stranded on a desert island and could only eat one fruit each day for the rest of eternity, it would be the fig, for its sweetness and beauty. Figs are held in high esteem in Greece: they are a daily staple and can be found on mezze platters, salads, dipped in chocolate, stuffed with cheeses or nuts, part of breakfast cereals and cakes, being made into jams and preserves, mixed into pastas or dried for daily use.

The figs were introduced to Ancient Greece from Egypt in the 9th century BC. To the Ancient Greeks, the fig symbolised peace and prosperity. They were so revered in the region of Attica that their ruler in ancient times, Solon, made it illegal to export the fig to other countries so as to ensure they were reserved only for its people.

Line your serving bowl with basil or sorrel leaves (or both) and drizzle with either a little pomegranate molasses or balsamic glaze.

Gently place the fig halves on top of the leaves (don't toss to combine as it's nice to see the figs on top). Crumble over goat's cheese and add the almonds, pomegranate seeds and a drizzle of honey.

MAKE IT VEGAN

By using maple, date or dandelion syrup, vegan honey or agave nectar instead of honey, and a vegan feta and goat's cheese.

MAKE IT GLUTEN-FREE

It already is!

WHAT TO DO WITH LEFTOVERS

All the ingredients in this salad would make for terrific toppings on a pizza (trying drizzling some honey on it too for extra sweetness and to open the flavours).

Σαλάτα Χόρτα με πατάτες και κολοκυθάκια

Horta salad with potatoes and zucchini

SERVES 6

1 tablespoon rock salt

1 kg silverbeet (Swiss chard), chicory or other greens, trimmed, washed and chopped

2 large potatoes, quartered and boiled for 15–20 minutes, or until soft in the centre

2 large zucchinis (courgettes), cut into very thick slices and boiled for 8 minutes

60 ml (2 fl oz/¼ cup) extra-virgin olive oil

juice of 1 lemon

salt and pepper, to taste

1 teaspoon Greek oregano

2 tablespoons white vinegar

50 g (1¾ oz) Greek feta

The beauty of this dish is that you can use any greens you have to hand, or that are growing in your garden. Dandelion greens, amaranth greens, silverbeet (Swiss chard), sorrel greens or any other long-stemmed robust green leaf, washed and roughly chopped, will work really well in this dish. If you are using wild Greek greens instead of sweeter ones such as silverbeet, to get rid of the bitterness, boil the greens for 10 minutes and then drain the water and fill a fresh pot and continue boiling for another 10–15 minutes.

Fill a large saucepan three-quarters full with water. Add rock salt and bring to the boil.

Add the silverbeet (or other greens), potatoes and zucchini, bring the water back to the boil, then reduce to a simmer and cook for 25–30 minutes.

Drain well, squeezing out excess water, then transfer to a bowl. There is no need to chop them again.

Add olive oil, lemon juice, salt and pepper, Greek oregano and vinegar and toss to combine. Sprinkle with feta, if you like, to serve.

MAKE IT VEGAN

By using a vegan feta.

MAKE IT GLUTEN-FREE

It already is!

WHAT TO DO WITH LEFTOVERS

This salad will keep well for 2–3 days if refrigerated and stored in an airtight container, or you can drain and squeeze the greens of their juices, roughly chop and make a fantastic omelette or scrambled eggs with them. If you are into wheatgrass shots and the like, look no further – save the juices from the horta, pour them into a jug with a little salt and drink.

Σαλάτα με καρπούζι και ούζο

Watermelon and ouzo salad

SERVES 4

¼ watermelon (about 125 g/4½ oz), peeled and sliced into chunks

30 ml (1 fl oz) ouzo

1 red onion, sliced into thin rings

50 g (1¾ oz) Greek feta, crumbled

2 tablespoons roughly chopped mint

½ bunch basil, torn

Watermelon has been valued by the Greeks for a few thousand years, not just as a culinary delight but also as a diuretic and a medical treatment for heatstroke (they recommended placing the wet rind of the watermelon on one's forehead). Today, watermelon is used copiously in fruit platters and salads, as well as being fried as fritters, baked as a part of cakes and sweets or cooked into delicious glyko karpouzi as a sweet preserve.

Place watermelon in a large bowl and pour over the ouzo. Leave the ouzo to soak into the cut watermelon for a few hours in the fridge to help create a delicious, intense flavour.

Gently toss the watermelon with all remaining ingredients together in a large bowl.

MAKE IT VEGAN

By using a vegan feta.

MAKE IT GLUTEN-FREE

It already is!

WHAT TO DO WITH LEFTOVERS

Take out the onions and blend everything else with some ice cubes and extra ouzo to make a delicious watermelon ouzo shake.

Πατατοσαλάτα

Patata salata

SERVES 6

4 large potatoes, peeled
finely grated zest of ¼ lemon
2 tablespoons white vinegar
1 teaspoon Greek oregano
salt and pepper, to taste
1 onion, sliced into rings
juice of 1 lemon
15 g (½ oz/½ cup) flat-leaf
    (Italian) parsley, chopped
30 g (1 oz/½ cup) dill,
    chopped
extra-virgin olive oil, for
    drizzling
1 spring onion (scallion),
    finely sliced
2 tablespoons capers

The humble potato is believed to have been introduced to Greece in 1822 thanks to the first governor of Independent Greece, Ioannis Kapodistrias, after the Greeks rose up and reclaimed their country after 400 years of occupation at the hands of Turkey and reclaimed their country. Greece had been economically ravaged and he introduced potato farming as a way to improve the standard of living, due to the affordability and ease of growing this vegetable in the Greek climate. The island of Naxos is now most famous for its potatoes, growing more than eight million kilograms a year and having an annual potato festival to celebrate them!

Bring a large saucepan of water to the boil. Add potatoes and cook for 10–15 minutes, depending on the size of the potatoes, until tender but still firm. You do not want the potatoes to become too soft or mushy. Set aside until cool enough to handle, then slice into quarters and add to a large bowl.

Add lemon zest, vinegar, Greek oregano and season to taste with salt and pepper. Add onion rings and lemon juice and season again. Add parsley and dill and drizzle with extra-virgin olive oil. Add spring onion and capers and toss everything together.

MAKE IT VEGAN

It already is!

MAKE IT GLUTEN-FREE

It already is!

WHAT TO DO WITH LEFTOVERS

Blend the leftovers together with a little milk to make a delicious mash for lunch the next day.

Πατζαροσαλάτα

Beetroot salad

SERVES 6

4 fresh beetroot (beet), with
    leaves cut off and reserved
4 garlic cloves, sliced
1 spring onion (scallion),
    sliced
10 g (¼ oz/¼ cup) flat-leaf
    (Italian) parsley
20 g (¾ oz/⅓ cup) dill,
    chopped
Greek-style yoghurt
    (optional), to serve
2 tablespoons white vinegar
4 tablespoon extra-virgin
    olive oil
salt and pepper, to taste

Beetroot (beet) is such a versatile vegetable and one that is deeply under-appreciated. Most know it only as something sliced that comes out of a tin. Fresh is truly always best when it comes to beetroot. Roasted or boiled, it is divine. When boiling, make sure to keep the leaves, as they make for an incredible salad when tossed with a little extra-virgin olive oil and white vinegar. This salad is vegan and also free from nuts, but you could add walnuts and almonds if you like, or crumble over some feta or goat's cheese, or even place on a bed of labneh.

Peel the beetroots and cut into quarters. I personally never use gloves as a good wash with warm water will get the beetroot colour off your hands pretty easily but if you want to avoid needing to do this, wear some kitchen gloves while peeling and cutting the beetroot.

Bring a large saucepan of water to the boil, and cook beetroot for 10 minutes. Add reserved beetroot leaves and continue to boil for another 15 minutes, or until tender. Drain.

Arrange beetroot leaves first on a serving platter then add the beetroot pieces, and top with garlic, spring onion and herbs.

Drizzle generously with extra-virgin olive oil and white vinegar, and season with salt and pepper to taste. You can also add dollops of yoghurt to serve, if you like.

MAKE IT VEGAN

It already is! If you use yoghurt, just use coconut yoghurt.

MAKE IT GLUTEN-FREE

It already is!

WHAT TO DO WITH LEFTOVERS

Place leftovers into a blender and blend on low speed to create a delicious beetroot (beet) dip.

RESISTANCE

My Greek ancestors have seen it all, from world wars to invasions and the rise and fall of fascism.

Greeks have endured annexation by the Roman Empire, invasions by the Persian Empire, 400 years of occupation at the hands of the Ottoman Empire, our ancient wonders of the world being burnt to the ground or destroyed by wars, our Parthenon (Elgin) marbles being stolen, the Pontian genocide at the hands of Turkey, the rise of a fascist military junta in the 1960s and the economic crises of this century. Still, our culture thrives and can be found around the globe, through our diaspora of immigrants and refugees. Through it all, Greeks have not lost their hearts, humanity, or their spirit of welcome.

This history makes me proud and connects me to my culture, and has helped form my identity. I reflect on the resilience, strength and courage of my ancestors and how they have influenced me. What has resisted and survived beyond all that we Greeks have experienced – and even more impressive than the wonder of the Parthenon and Acropolis – is our ability to share knowledge, culture and teachings with the world, from democracy, political science and mathematics to the art of gathering around a meal as family, and as community, sharing food, recipes and stories.

The food of Greece has inevitably helped shape the food culture of those who occupied us, as well as those who traded with us. And as colonisers or neighbours, we too have been influenced by the food culture of those around us. Our food, for example, has roots in Afroasiatic cultures, the legacy of people such as Pythagoras undertaking studies in Egypt and bringing back to Greece some of their favourite recipes. At the same time, we Greeks shared some of our beloved fare, with sweets such as halva and baklava being as easy to find in Cairo these days as it is in Athens.

My grandparents survived two world wars. On my father's side, they survived a Nazi occupation, during which they were forced to flee their homelands as refugees, with whatever they could carry in their hands. On my mother's side, the rise of fascism would result in my grandfather regularly having to go into hiding after being accused by the junta of being a communist. No matter how poor or how persecuted our people and our culture, our food has survived and the Greek diaspora has filled the world with its magic.

We rarely think of it as this, but food is deeply political. It is a social armour that migrants and refugees use to safely integrate in new lands. It is also an act of defiance against oppressors and those who seek to assimilate and erase us. As long as our food, language and stories survive, and are passed on to the next generation, then so too do we survive. We have prevailed and triumphed and bent the arc of humanity back towards us.

Migrants and refugees hold on fiercely to their food culture. It is one of the few things that can survive war, displacement and oppression and still find root in foreign soil, helping forge new beginnings. When our food is embraced, so too is a part of us, and as it is shared, the seeds of new roots that allow us to call these new shores home spread also.

The migrant and refugee story always has food at its heart. This cultural heritage is an

Begin, be bold, and venture to be wise.

– HORACE

act of defiance and resistance as much as it is an act of celebration.

Often, as my parents experienced when they first arrived in Australia, many migrants and refugees are not welcomed. My parents would tell me about how they were abused and told to go back to where they came from, how relatives were spat at and beaten up for being Greek. This was a story that also echoed through my childhood when I was growing up in country Australia.

Migrants and refugees use food to disarm our oppressors. We know it's a safe entry point to our cultures and there are few cities, regional or rural towns where you will not find a Chinese, Thai, Indian or kebab restaurant. Where our struggle often lies is that while our food is welcomed, we are not – and the pressure to assimilate is immense.

We carry our food with us, as we do our language, memories and ancestry. It forms part of our promise to pass on our culture and stories to the next generation so we do not disappear in the sands of struggle and assimilation. We share our food so proudly and each meal is a tribute to our cultural roots and ancestors.

Μαρουλοσαλάτα

Maroulosalata | Lettuce salad

SERVES 4

1 whole iceberg lettuce, very thinly sliced

3 spring onions (scallions), thinly sliced

20 g (¾ oz/⅓ cup) mint, chopped

20 g (¾ oz/⅓ cup) flat-leaf (Italian) parsley, chopped

20 g (¾ oz/⅓ cup) dill, chopped

1 tomato, diced

1 red onion, sliced

DRESSING

1 lemon

3 tablespoons white vinegar

4 tablespoons extra-virgin olive oil

salt and pepper, to taste

Every time my mum, Sia, makes this salad, I am left in wonder at how something so simple with so few ingredients can taste so incredible. The leftovers taste even better, as the juices, oils and flavours deepen with time.

So if ever you need proof of how simple, fresh ingredients can create something wonderful, look no further than this salad. It is a staple of most Greek lunch and dinner tables, as it's a simple, affordable dish that at its heart relies simply on lettuce. You can use any type of lettuce – the key is to slice it as finely as you can.

Combine lettuce, spring onion, mint, parsley, dill, tomato and red onion in a large bowl. Add lemon juice, white vinegar and olive oil and season to taste. Toss to combine.

MAKE IT VEGAN

It already is!

MAKE IT GLUTEN-FREE

It already is!

WHAT TO DO WITH LEFTOVERS

You can quickly repurpose this into another salad by combining it with more quartered tomatoes, sliced cucumbers, pitted olives, capsicums (bell peppers) and Greek feta.

Κουκιά με αγκινάρες σε λεμόνι και ελαιόλαδο

Broad beans, artichokes in lemon and olive oil

SERVES 4

20 fresh broad beans in skin, podded
8 fresh, tinned or bottled artichoke hearts, halved
2 tablespoons chopped dill
1 tablespoon roughly chopped mint
½ fennel bulb, thinly sliced
1 teaspoon Greek oregano
1 spring onion (scallion), thinly sliced
juice of 1 lemon
3 tablespoons extra-virgin olive oil
salt and pepper, to taste

For more than 3000 years, Greeks have been creating mouthwatering salads, stews, baked dishes and mezzes with the artichoke. It has a special place in Greek culture – in our mythology it was considered food for the gods of Olympus and has such an ancient history because it was prized by Ancient Greek healers for its potent medicinal properties. The origin story is that Zeus fell in love with a beautiful woman named Cynara, whom he then banished back to the mortal world when his love was not reciprocated, turning her into a wild thorny artichoke plant. Cynara is the botanical name for artichokes.

Bring a small saucepan of water to the boil. Add broad beans and cook for 5 minutes, or until tender. Drain and set aside.

Combine broad beans with artichoke, dill, mint, fennel, Greek oregano and spring onion. Stir in lemon juice, dress with olive oil and season to taste.

MAKE IT VEGAN

It already is!

MAKE IT GLUTEN-FREE

It already is!

WHAT TO DO WITH LEFTOVERS

Make them into a delicious frittata by placing in a baking dish with cream, crumbled feta, milk and beaten eggs and bake till golden. Or mix leftovers with beaten egg and crumbled feta, grated halloumi or kasseri and cook like an omelette.

Λεωνίδας Χωριάτικη σαλάτα

Leo's Greek salad

SERVES 4

4 ripe red tomatoes, peeled
  and diced
1 red or green capsicum
  (bell pepper), deseeded
  and sliced
100 g (3½ oz) pitted
  Kalamata olives
1 red onion, sliced or diced
3 spring onion (scallions),
  sliced
1 cucumber, sliced
60 g (2 oz) capers (optional)
1 teaspoon Greek oregano
100 g (3½ oz) Greek feta
extra-virgin olive oil, to taste
1 tablespoon white vinegar

When I think about making a Greek salad, I think about my dad, Leo, and how much I miss him. I so deeply wish he was here now sharing this dish with me over a few cold beers on a warm summer night in his magical garden.

As I have mentioned, my dad would take so much pride in making the most heavenly Greek salads for us from tomatoes he had home-grown in the summer months, with all the fresh herbs from his garden, too. The key to my dad's magical tomato salads was using the freshest and most ripe tomatoes, onions sliced into rings, and being very, very generous with the amount of Greek feta, salt and extra-virgin olive oil he would add. Leo knew that a great Greek salad needed lots of oils and juices to make the most of the tomato's summer ripeness. He would mix the feta and tomatoes with his hands, then mix in the Greek oregano and give the salad the olive oil it needed for one to be able to dip bread into its juices for days to come.

Using your hands, combine tomato, capsicum, olives, red onion, spring onion, cucumber, capers (if using), Greek oregano and feta in a large bowl. Drizzle generously with extra-virgin olive oil and toss with the vinegar to serve.

MAKE IT VEGAN

By using a vegan feta.

MAKE IT GLUTEN-FREE

It already is!

WHAT TO DO WITH LEFTOVERS

A Greek salad is even better the next day as all the juices of the tomatoes have mixed with the feta and other ingredients. My best advice for leftovers is to actually just add more tomatoes, feta, capsicum (bell peppers) and cucumbers to the existing bowl of leftovers, as you get an even more flavoursome Greek salad.

Σαλάτα με μάραθο

Fennel salad

SERVES 4

2 fennel bulbs, trimmed
    and thinly sliced
60 g (2 oz) dill, chopped
juice of 1 lemon
1 spring onion (scallion),
    sliced
3 tablespoons extra-virgin
    olive oil
salt and pepper, to taste

We love fennel in Greek cooking. We use it both as a herb and a vegetable to give our dishes that sweet aniseed flavour. Fennel is native to Greece, growing on our beaches, and in our lakes and rivers. It's an ingredient we have used for thousands of years. It has a special place in Greek mythology too, the tale being that when Prometheus stole fire from the gods to give to humankind, he did so by using a fennel stalk to hold the fire before giving his gift to humanity. This salad is spring in a bowl and is ready in less than five minutes, with the fresh, full flavour of the fennel unlocked by slicing it very thinly and mixing it with dill and lemon.

Combine all ingredients in a large bowl and season well with salt and pepper. That's it!

MAKE IT VEGAN

It already is!

MAKE IT GLUTEN-FREE

It already is!

WHAT TO DO WITH LEFTOVERS

Fresh fennel is great in almost any salad, so repurpose it into a new salad with tomatoes, cucumbers, feta, capsicums (bell peppers), add some fresh mint too and finish with extra-virgin olive oil.

Vegetables
& Soups

Αυγολέμονο

Avgolemono | Egg and lemon soup

SERVES 6

200 g (7 oz/1 cup) medium-
grain rice, rinsed and dried
2 vegan stock cubes (chicken
flavoured)
40 g (1½ oz) butter
2 litres (2½ fl oz) cold water,
plus 2 teaspoons extra
1 teaspoon salt
3 small eggs, separated
salt and pepper, to season
juice of 2–3 lemons (or more
to taste)

This is the soup of my childhood. I remember every time I was sick with a cold or flu this would be the soup my mum would make for me. Simply eating this soup would make me feel less sick. It is the lemony warmth of this soup, with that beautiful egg lemon froth on top, that you feel in your tummy with each spoonful. When you make this soup, make sure to crack lots of pepper all over it as for the perfect finishing touch.

Wash the rice in a colander for a minute and let it dry.

Combine rice, stock cubes and butter in a large pot and cover with the water. Bring to the boil, then reduce to a simmer. Add salt and cook for 15 minutes until the soup is creamy but neither thick nor watery (you still want a soupy consistency, so don't reduce it too much). If your soup thickens too much, add a little extra water. Remove from heat.

Essential to making this soup so delicious is a thick egg lemon froth that is poured on top of the finished soup. We make this by combining egg whites with 1 teaspoon of water in a large bowl and, using a small hand mixer, beating until the mixture becomes stiff like you are making meringue. Slowly add in the yolks, continuing to mix until combined. Gradually pour in the lemon juice and continue mixing for another minute. Take 3 ladles of the soup mixture and add it to this bowl and mix for another minute. Then pour this mixture evenly over the top of the soup. Stir it through once using the soup ladle.

Plate and serve with salt and a generous amount of cracked pepper. If you want an even more lemony flavoured soup, you can squeeze more lemon onto your soup to finish.

MAKE IT VEGAN

Use a vegan egg mix and vegan butter.

MAKE IT GLUTEN-FREE

It already is!

WHAT TO DO WITH LEFTOVERS

This soup is even better the next day with some toasted cubed bread mixed in.

Φασολάδα

Fasolatha | White bean and tomato soup

SERVES 6

500 g (1 lb 2 oz) dried
    cannellini beans or great
    northern beans
80 ml (2½ fl oz/⅓ cup)
    extra-virgin olive oil
2 brown or red onions,
    finely diced
3 garlic cloves, finely diced
3 sticks of celery, skinned
    and finely chopped
3 carrots, finely diced
1 tablespoon tomato paste
200 g (7 oz) tinned crushed
    tomatoes or diced tomatoes
1 bay leaf
3 cloves
salt and pepper, to taste
1 teaspoon salt
crusty bread, olives and feta,
    to serve

My father, Leo, used to love making this for me and my sister; he took such joy in it. Back home from a long day working at a factory, he would still patiently cook this comfort soup for us. It was watching my dad make this that taught me that a man's place can be in the kitchen. This is my favourite soup. It's divine comfort food for the soul anytime and makes me think of my dad, Leo, every time I have it.

Bring a large pot of water to the boil, add beans and cook for 30 minutes. Drain and wash in a colander and set aside.

Return the pot to a low heat, add olive oil and onion and cook for 2 minutes. Add the garlic and fry for another 2 minutes, add the celery and carrots and fry for another 5 minutes.

Add the beans in and stir for a few minutes, then add the tomato paste and tinned tomato and stir through.

Cover the mixture generously with water and add the bay leaf and cloves.

Bring to the boil, then reduce to a simmer and cook on low heat for about 90 minutes until beans are tender and the soup is creamy but not watery.

Add the teaspoon of salt at the end, to taste (with about 5 minutes to go. Don't add salt at the start when cooking bean soups as beans will never cook properly).

Serve with crusty bread, olives and feta.

MAKE IT VEGAN

It already is!

MAKE IT GLUTEN-FREE

It already is!

WHAT TO DO WITH LEFTOVERS

Will keep well refrigerated for up to 5 days. You can also blend up the leftovers with a stick blender to create a new texture.

Ρεβύθια

Revithia | Chickpea soup

SERVES 4

500 g (1 lb 2 oz) dried
  chickpeas (garbanzos),
  soaked overnight in cold
  water (make sure to
  generously completely
  cover them with water)
80 ml (2½ fl oz/⅓ cup)
  extra-virgin olive oil
2 red onions, diced
3 sticks celery, diced
2 garlic cloves, finely diced
2 large carrots, diced
1 sprig rosemary
1 bay leaf
1 tablespoon plain
  (all-purpose) flour
juice of 2 lemons
1 teaspoon Greek oregano
salt and pepper, to taste
extra lemon, extra-virgin olive
  oil and Greek oregano to
  garnish

This is a gorgeous vegan chickpea soup that originates from the Greek island of Sifnos, where this soup is had on Sundays, as it was made in the embers of the still-hot wood oven from the previous Saturday night. You can thicken this soup by adding flour, as I explain below, or by using tahini.

Drain and wash the soaked chickpeas and place in a fresh pot of water. Bring to the boil then reduce to a simmer and cook for 30 minutes. Drain and wash and set aside to help get rid of the white fluff that comes from cooking chickpeas.

Heat olive oil in a large pot over a low heat and sauté the onions for 2 minutes to soften. Add celery and cook for a further 2 minutes, then add the garlic, carrot, rosemary sprig and bay leaf and cook for a further 5 minutes to caramelise.

Next add all the chickpeas and, using a wooden spoon, mix them thoroughly through all the other ingredients and cook for a couple of minutes. Add enough water to generously fully cover the chickpeas.

Bring to boil and then reduce to low heat to simmer for about 90 minutes – you want the chickpeas to be soft and tender but not mushy and for the juices to significantly reduce.

Now, using a soup ladle, scoop 2 ladles of the soup into a small food processor and blend for a couple of seconds. Add lemon juice and flour to help thicken the soup and blend for a couple more seconds. Don't blend too finely – we want a thick soup.

Return mixture to the soup. Ladle into serving bowls, season to taste and sprinkle with Greek oregano and extra olive oil to serve. Add more lemon juice if you want it extra tangy!

MAKE IT VEGAN
  It already is!

MAKE IT GLUTEN-FREE
  Use a gluten-free flour.

WHAT TO DO WITH LEFTOVERS
  You can drain the juices in
  a colander and blend into a
  lemony hummus-style dip.

Τραχανάς

Trahana soup

SERVES 4

1 teaspoon sugar
200 g (7 oz) tinned crushed
    tomatoes
1 tablespoon tomato paste
½ teaspoon sweet paprika
3 cloves
½ teaspoon nutmeg
½ teaspoon cinnamon
1 vegetable stock cube
salt and pepper, to taste
1.25 litres (42 fl oz/5 cups)
    water
300 g (10½ oz/2 cups) sour
    trahana
100 g (3½ oz) Greek feta and/
    or Greek-style yoghurt, to
    serve
80 ml (2½ fl oz/⅓ cup)
    extra-virgin olive oil
thick slice of bread, to serve
    (optional)

Trahana is a traditional Greek grain, made with either semolina, cracked wheat or flour. It comes both in a sweet (made with sheep's or goat's milk) and sour (made with soured milk and/or yoghurt) form. In Ancient Greek times, this dish was prepared as a way of preserving milk for the harsh, cold winter months. You can buy trahana from any Mediterranean deli or make it yourself. You can make both a tomato version, as I have here, or a sketo version (that is, one without tomato), which instead of the tomatoes uses lemon, olive oil and vegetable stock.

Combine sugar, tomatoes, tomato paste, spices, vegetable stock cube, salt and pepper and water in a large pot over medium heat. Bring to the boil, then reduce to a simmer and cook for 10 minutes. Add trahana and return to the boil, then reduce to a simmer and cook for another 15–20 minutes, stirring regularly, until you get a creamy consistency. You can enjoy it just like this or serve with Greek feta crumbled over and drizzlings of extra-virgin olive oil. You can also substitute the Greek feta with Greek yoghurt. If you like, serve with a thick slice of bread.

MAKE IT VEGAN

Use vegan feta.

MAKE IT GLUTEN-FREE

By using a gluten-free trahana.

WHAT TO DO WITH LEFTOVERS

Leftover soup can be reheated the next day (refrigerate it until then) and add toasted cubed bread into the soup with more feta and olive oil.

JOY

I wanted to create a book that celebrates the magnificent culinary history of plant-based recipes in Greek culture that are barely known or profiled. My wish is to challenge people's ideas of Greek food and show how healthy, sustainable and inclusive it can be. Greek food is far more than kebabs, calamari and lamb on the spit. Vegetables rather than meat are at the heart of any Greek table and the Greeks were some of the earliest vegetarians and vegans in recorded human history.

In fact it wasn't until 1847 that the term 'vegetarian' was coined; until then a person who did not eat meat was said to be on the Pythagorean diet, named after the Greek philosopher Pythagoras.

To the Ancient Greeks, strict vegetarianism was called 'abstinence from beings with a soul' and was a well-known practice in those times. In ancient Athens, during the feast of Pyanopsia, there was a bloodless sacrifice of nuts and fruits, rather than the sacrifice of animals, to honour the god Apollo.

Polyspori (poly means many and spori means seeds) was the name given to vegan food traditionally prepared for Greek gods in return for them protecting the harvest. The Greek Orthodox religion has 40 days of Lenten fasting before Easter that calls on us to go vegan for this period of time each year.

Greek food is seen as heart-healthy, high in vegetables, fruits, legumes and unprocessed grains. Health professionals have consistently found it to be one of the healthiest diets in the world. A Mediterranean diet is believed to be linked to lower rates of cancer and cardiovascular ailments. It is a diet low in saturated fats, sugars and red meats and one high in beans, nuts and legumes.

Furthermore, a Greek diet has been found to help lower cholesterol and also reduce inflammation in the body. Some medical studies have also found that a Mediterranean diet is linked to a reduced risk of Parkinson's, Alzheimer's, and type 2 diabetes.

Greek olive oil is at the heart of all Greek cooking. I cook primarily with extra-virgin olive oil instead of vegetable or canola oil in all of my savoury cooking (the only exceptions are when I am frying chips, fritters or burgers).

Unripe grape gets sweet as honey, at a slow pace.
– GREEK PROVERB

Olive oil is a far healthier option, rich in healthy omega-3 fatty acids, and extra-virgin olive oil is even better. Rich in carotenoids and polyphenols, it has antioxidant and anti-inflammatory properties.

Everything you will find on a traditional Greek kitchen table at dinner time can be considered community on a plate: from the delicious Kalamata olives that one devours by the handful, which are rich in antioxidants, to Greek greens such as silverbeet (Swiss chard), which are rich in carotenoids, vitamin C, magnesium, iron and calcium.

The lemons that dress so many of the recipes in my book help provide an acidity that lowers glycemic response. The lemon zest in my Greek potatoes is high in flavonoid content, which has a beneficial impact on blood glucose, helping to control or prevent diabetes.

The garlic that is found throughout most of my recipes has great antioxidant and anti-inflammatory effects. Fresh mint, dill and parsley not only add great flavour to so many of these dishes, but also contain anti-oxidant and anti-inflammatory compounds, especially polyphenols and flavonols.

The Greek feta that is served at every meal I have with my family, along with a side of Greek-style yoghurt, provides some of the best probiotics you can enjoy and offers much needed protein to vegans and vegetarians.

This is pure food, food that is good for the body, heart and soul. At a time when everything feels fast, transient and disposable, where big supermarkets pre-cut our fruit and wrap it in packaging, and our salads come in plastic instead of from the soil, how we imagine food and where it comes from, the knowledge of how to grow it, nurture it and connect to it is gradually erased from our collective memory.

We feel more stretched and time poor than ever before and turn to fast food to help ameliorate this. Yet the food we are often consuming is not feeding us what we actually need; it's starving us of it. We are faced with artificial ingredients, enhancements with indecipherable numerical codes on our packages, and a vacuous promise it will help create a better me, a better you. Yet after the initial hit and high, we often feel even more disconnected from our bodies and ourselves.

Let's replace fast food with heart food: nurturing food that is made with heart. This is the Greek way. Let's embrace it.

Φακές

Fakes | Lentil soup

SERVES 6

500 g brown lentils
80 ml (2½ fl oz/⅓ cup)
    extra-virgin olive oil
2 red or brown onions, diced
2 leeks, finely diced
2 carrots, finely diced
2 garlic cloves, finely diced
3 cloves
2 bay leaves
1 tablespoon tomato paste
200 g (2½ fl oz) tinned
    tomatoes or 2 fresh
    tomatoes, diced
50 g (1¾ oz) long-grain rice
    (optional)
1 teaspoon Greek oregano
salt and pepper, to taste
2 tablespoons white vinegar
olives, feta and bread,
    to serve

This is the go-to soup for all Greeks. Healthy, nutritious, hearty, cheap and easy to make, it is a soup for any season or time of day and is full of fibre, potassium, protein and iron. I love it with some extra white vinegar, olive oil and some diced onion on top. My father, Leo, used to love making it for my sister, Nola, and I. He would cook it slowly on low heat, with so much love and care for us. Once again, it was his way of showing his love for us when he didn't have the words to express it.

Place lentils and enough water to cover them in a large pot of water. Bring to the boil, then reduce heat to a simmer and cook for 5 minutes. Drain and set aside (this will reduce the bitterness of the lentils).

Heat oil in a large pot or saucepan over a low heat. Add onion, leek, carrot and garlic and cook for 10 minutes.

Add the lentils to the pot of fried vegetables and add cloves, bay leaves, tomato paste and tinned tomatoes. You can add the rice at this point if you would like a thicker soup. Add enough water to cover the lentils by at least 10 cm/4 in (if the lentils absorb all the water before they are cooked, add a little more).

Bring to the boil and then reduce heat to simmer on low heat. Cook for 30–40 minutes, or until lentils become creamy and the soup has a thick texture. Season to taste with salt, pepper and a splash of white vinegar. Sprinkle with more olive oil and Greek oregano. Serve with olives, feta cheese and bread.

MAKE IT VEGAN

It already is!

MAKE IT GLUTEN-FREE

It already is!

WHAT TO DO WITH LEFTOVERS

Drain the fakes in a colander, place in a bowl with eggs, breadcrumbs and flour and make into lentil patties to fry until golden.

Στιφάδο με μανιτάρια πεύκου

Pine mushroom stew

SERVES 4

250 g (9 oz) pine mushrooms
90 ml (3 fl oz) extra-virgin
    olive oil
1 brown or red onion
3 garlic cloves, finely chopped
60 ml (2 fl oz/¼ cup) shiraz
    wine
250 g (9 oz) silverbeet
    (Swiss chard) or spinach
1 teaspoon sweet paprika
200 g (7 oz) tinned crushed
    tomatoes
1 tablespoon tomato paste
250 ml (8½ fl oz/1 cup) water
salt and pepper, to taste

Greece is renowned for its wild mushrooms. There are in fact 2400 species of mushrooms, 150 of which are edible. The most popular include morel and chanterelle mushrooms. We forage for them everywhere, by farms, forests, lakes and rivers.

Greeks have always appreciated the deliciousness of mushrooms, not just for their culinary wonder but also for their mind-altering properties. The Ancient Greeks would enjoy the psychedelic effects of wild mushrooms, indulging in them at festivals that would go for days. Hippocrates would teach his students of their healing properties.

Of all of my mum Sia's creations, this recipe is unique; she uses pine mushrooms with wonderful greens to create this heavenly stew. At Easter, I think this dish could make a wonderful vegan alternative to the dreaded magiritsa soup, the offal stew that's traditionally served on Holy Saturday.

Clean pine mushrooms thoroughly and bring a medium saucepan of water to the boil. Add mushrooms and cook for 5 minutes on a high heat. Drain and thickly slice, then set aside.

Heat olive oil in a large pot over a low heat.

Add onion and fry for 2 minutes. Add garlic and fry for a further 2 minutes, then add red wine and cook for about 3–4 minutes, or until liquid is reduced.

Add silverbeet and continue cooking for about 5 minutes, or until the leaves wilt.

Add mushrooms and fry for another 5 minutes.

Add sweet paprika, tomato, tomato paste and water and season with salt and pepper. Bring mixture to the boil, then reduce to a simmer and cook for a further 15 minutes until sauce thickens. Serve.

MAKE IT VEGAN

It already is!

MAKE IT GLUTEN-FREE

It already is!

WHAT TO DO WITH LEFTOVERS

Enjoy with some boiled or fried rice the next day.

Μουσακάς

Moussaka

SERVES 6

1 litre (34 fl oz) canola oil,
    for frying
3 large potatoes, sliced
2 large eggplants
    (aubergines), sliced
2 large zucchinis (courgettes),
    sliced
300 g (10½ oz/2 cups) kasseri
    cheese, coarsely grated
35 g (1¼ oz/⅓ cup) mizithra,
    finely grated
½ teaspoon freshly grated
    nutmeg

TOMATO SAUCE
120 ml (4 fl oz) extra-virgin
    olive oil
1 onion, finely diced
1 teaspoon sugar
3 garlic cloves, finely diced
2 carrots, grated
1 zucchini (courgette), grated
700 g (1 lb 9 oz) mushrooms,
    roughly chopped
400 g (14 oz) tinned crushed
    tomatoes
1 tablespoon tomato paste
3 cloves, crushed
800 ml (27 fl oz) water
½ teaspoon freshly grated
    nutmeg
½ teaspoon sweet paprika
½ teaspoon cinnamon
10 g (¼ oz/½ cup) mint, finely
    chopped
30 g (1 oz/½ cup) dill, finely
    chopped
15 g (½ oz/½ cup) flat-leaf
    (Italian) parsley,
    finely chopped
salt and pepper, to taste

Moussaka takes its name from the Arabic word 'musaqqa'ah' and was created when Arabs introduced eggplants (aubergines) to Greece. It is a beloved dish in Greek cooking, a dish we especially make at Easter and Christmas time to share with loved ones, and whenever we are looking for hearty comfort food at its best. I love eating this warm from the oven, and even cold the next day when it somehow tastes even better.

Heat canola oil in a large frying pan over a high heat until hot. Add the sliced vegetables, in batches, and cook until golden and brown, taking care not to burn, as that flavour will permeate the dish. (Don't put too many vegetable slices into the frying pan at the same time as they won't fry properly.) Once cooked, transfer to a paper towel and set aside for at least 15 minutes to drain excess oil.

TO MAKE THE TOMATO SAUCE

Heat the oil in a large frying pan over a medium heat and sauté the onion and sugar for about 3 minutes, stirring until caramelised. Add the garlic and fry for a couple more minutes, then add the carrot and zucchini and fry for another 5 minutes. Add the mushroom and cook for a further 5 minutes. Reduce heat to low and add the tinned tomatoes, tomato paste, cloves, water and spices, and cook for a further 5 minutes. Add herbs and cook for another 15–20 minutes to get a nice thick sauce (you do not want it to be watery). Season with salt and pepper.

TO MAKE THE BÉCHAMEL SAUCE

To make the béchamel sauce, melt the butter in a medium-sized pot, then gradually add the flour and stir constantly until it thickens and forms a paste. Gradually add the milk, stirring constantly over a medium heat until it thickens into a thick sauce. Stir through the grated kasseri and mizithra, crack eggs in and stir through. Season with pepper.

BÉCHAMEL SAUCE

250 g (9 oz) unsalted butter

90 g (3 oz) plain (all-purpose) flour

1.5 litres (51 fl oz/6 cups) milk

150g (5½ oz/1 cup) kasseri cheese, grated

40g (1½ oz/⅓ cup) mizithra, finely grated

2 eggs

pepper, to taste

TO ASSEMBLE THE DISH

Preheat the oven to 200°C (390°F). Brush a rectangular 3 litre (101 fl oz/12 cup) capacity ovenproof dish with oil to lightly grease, and spread a little tomato sauce and béchamel sauce over the bottom of the dish. Top with a layer of fried vegetables (mix up the vegetables rather than using a layer of just potatoes, for example) and sprinkle over half the kasseri cheese.

Repeat with another layer of tomato sauce, a little béchamel sauce, mixed vegetables and cheese.

Add a third layer of fried vegetables.

Pour remaining béchamel sauce over the top and finish with grated nutmeg and mizithra.

Cook for 45 minutes, then reduce oven temperature to 180°C (360°F) and cook for a further 35–40 minutes until you get a golden brown crust.

Now as hard as this is, let the dish sit for at least 1 hour at room temperature before you cut it to serve, so that it holds its shape. If you cut it straight out of the oven, it will lose its shape and you will not do all your hard work justice.

MAKE IT VEGAN

Replace the eggs with a vegan egg mix or leave out altogether and use a vegan butter, vegan cheeses and soy milk.

MAKE IT GLUTEN-FREE

Just use a gluten-free flour for the béchamel sauce.

WHAT TO DO WITH LEFTOVERS

When refrigerated, the leftovers can be enjoyed over the next 1–3 days. The flavours develop over time and become richer and more delicious.

Παπουτσάκια

Papoutsakia | Stuffed eggplant

SERVES 4

4 eggplants (aubergines)
salt, to taste
a few thyme sprigs, leaves
    picked
2 tablespoons extra-virgin
    olive oil
40 g (1½ oz/⅓ cup) mizithra,
    finely grated, to serve

TOMATO SAUCE
2 tablespoons extra-virgin
    olive oil
1 onion, grated
1 teaspoon sugar
3 garlic cloves, smashed
250 g (9 oz) chopped
    mushrooms
1 carrot, grated
1 zucchini (courgette), grated
15 g (2 oz/½ cup) flat-leaf
    (Italian) parsley, chopped
10 g (2 oz/½ cup) mint,
    chopped
60 g (2 oz/½ cup) basil,
    chopped
2 bay leaves
2 cloves
1 teaspoon vegetable stock
    powder
80 ml (2½ fl oz/⅓ cup) water
400 g (14½ oz) tinned diced
    tomatoes
1 cinnamon stick
1 tablespoon tomato paste
salt and pepper, to taste

Papoutsakia means 'little shoes' in Greek, which is a seriously cute name for a dish. It gets this name from the fact that these little parcels of béchamel, cheese and vegetable goodness are packaged in eggplants (aubergines; you can use regular or Lebanese) that look like little shoes. This is part of the lathera family of cooking, where olive oil is used plentifully to bring out the full flavour. You can also finish this dish with crumbled Greek feta or grated kasseri, kefalograviera or kefalotiri cheese.

Preheat the oven to 200°C (390°F). Slice each eggplant in half and cut criss-cross into the flesh to make mini diamond shapes. Place in a roasting tin (slice the bottom of each half of eggplant so it is flat and sits evenly on the base).

Season well with salt, sprinkle with thyme and drizzle with extra-virgin olive oil. Roast for 20 minutes until soft and golden. Set aside to cool slightly.

Meanwhile, make the tomato sauce. Heat olive oil in a frying pan over a medium heat and sauté the onion, sugar and garlic until soft.

Add the mushrooms and fry for 5 minutes.

Add the grated carrot and zucchini and fry for another 2 minutes.

Add all the fresh herbs, bay leaves, cloves, vegetable stock, water, tinned tomatoes, cinnamon stick and tomato paste and season with salt and pepper. Cook for about 30 minutes until you have no sauce juices left.

Once the eggplants are cool enough to handle, use a small spoon to gently scoop out the flesh from the middle of each eggplant half, leaving enough so the eggplant holds its shape. You can use your fingers to gently push any flesh to the sides of the eggplant halves so you have room for the sauce. Finely chop the scooped-out eggplant flesh and add to the tomato sauce and cook for a further 2 minutes.

BÉCHAMEL SAUCE

250 g (9 oz) unsalted butter

90 g (3 oz) plain (all-purpose) flour

1.5 litres (51 fl oz/6 cups) milk

150 g (5½ oz/1 cup) kasseri cheese, grated

40 g (1½ oz/⅓ cup) mizithra, finely grated

2 eggs

pepper, to taste

To make the béchamel sauce, melt the butter in a medium-sized pot, then gradually add the flour and stir constantly until it thickens and forms a paste. Gradually add the milk, stirring constantly over a medium heat until it thickens into a thick sauce. Now stir through the grated kasseri and mizithra, crack eggs in and stir through. Season with pepper.

Now fill each eggplant with your tomato sauce mixture and then dollop over the béchamel sauce (about 3 to 4 tablespoons per halved eggplant), covering the centre of the eggplant but not all of it so you can still see its outer line. Now sprinkle some grated mizithra all over each eggplant and bake for 40 minutes. If, after 40 minutes, the eggplants are not yet golden brown, place them under your oven grill on high for a couple of minutes. Keep a close eye on them to ensure they don't burn.

MAKE IT VEGAN

Replace the eggs with a vegan egg mix or leave out altogether and use a vegan butter.

MAKE IT GLUTEN-FREE

Use a gluten-free flour for the béchamel sauce.

WHAT TO DO WITH LEFTOVERS

Leftover eggplants (aubergines) can go towards making a fabulous melitzanosalata dip, or moussaka, as can the leftover béchamel.

Σκορδοστούμπι

Skordostoumbi | Baked eggplant

SERVES 6

5 large eggplants
  (aubergines), sliced into
  thick rounds
1 tablespoon salt
500 ml (17 fl oz/2 cups)
  canola oil, for frying
160 ml (5½ fl oz/⅔ cup)
  extra-virgin olive oil, plus
  extra for greasing
10 garlic cloves, finely sliced
8 large tomatoes, finely diced
salt and pepper, to taste
3 tablespoons red-wine
  vinegar or sherry vinegar
1 tablespoon honey
100 g (3½ oz) Greek feta,
  plus extra to serve
30 g (1 oz/1 cup) combined
  mint and flat-leaf (Italian)
  parsley, chopped

MAKE IT VEGAN

By using a vegan feta or by leaving feta out altogether.

MAKE IT GLUTEN-FREE

It already is!

WHAT TO DO WITH LEFTOVERS

Make a béchamel sauce to put on top of the leftovers and you have a mini eggplant (aubergine) moussaka or blend leftovers into a thick eggplant dip to enjoy.

There are so many dishes that are unique to different regions of Greece, and skordostoumbi is one that you will find on the Ionian Islands. Its name literally means 'stuffed with garlic'. Skordo is Greek for garlic and 'stoumbosame' is Greek slang for 'we are stuffed'. What is so unique about this dish is that it's made with 10 garlic cloves! Now don't hold back on the garlic – it makes the flavours so unique, especially when combined with the vinegar.

Place eggplant slices in a bowl, season with salt and cover with water. Set aside for 1 hour, then drain.

Heat 6 tablespoons of the canola oil in a large frying pan over a medium heat and cook eggplant slices, in batches and adding more canola oil as you go, for 2–3 minutes on each side or until golden. Set aside on a paper towel to drain the oil. (The eggplant is a very thirsty vegetable and will absorb a lot of the oil as you cook it so keep adding it to the pan).

To make the sauce, heat half the olive oil in a large frying pan over a medium heat. Add garlic and cook for a few minutes. Stir in tomatoes and season with salt and pepper. Bring the mixture to the boil, then reduce to a simmer and continue to cook for 5 minutes. Add honey and vinegar or sherry, then continue to cook for a further 20–30 minutes.

Preheat the oven to 170°C (340°F).

Brush a medium-sized oval or square roasting tin with olive oil and spoon a little of the tomato sauce into the base (I used a 31 cm/12¼ in × 23 cm/9 in × 5 cm (2 in) oval baking dish). Cover base with one layer of eggplant, then cover with a third of the sauce and crumble over half the feta and herbs. Add another layer of eggplant, another third of the sauce and the remaining feta and herbs. Finish with a layer of eggplant and the remaining sauce, pressing the mixture down gently with your hands. Drizzle with remaining extra-virgin olive oil and bake for 40–45 minutes. Cut into thick slices and serve with extra feta and herbs.

Μπριάμ

Briam | Roasted vegetables

SERVES 6

325 ml (11 fl oz/1½ cups)
  extra-virgin olive oil
400 g (14 oz) tinned crushed
  tomatoes
1 tablespoon tomato paste
4 garlic cloves, finely chopped
6 large potatoes, thinly sliced
2 tablespoons dried Greek
  oregano
1 teaspoon sweet paprika
50 g (1¾ oz/1 cup) mint,
  finely chopped
2 red or brown onions,
  finely sliced
3 large eggplants
  (aubergines), finely sliced
5 red, green or yellow
  capsicums (bell peppers),
  finely sliced
2 large zucchinis (courgettes),
  finely sliced
125 ml (4 fl oz/½ cup) water
3 sprigs rosemary, leaves
  picked
salt and pepper, to taste

Briam is comfort at its finest. We usually call it tourlou tourlou in Greek, referencing a delicious mix-up of vegetables. Its joy is in its simplicity – it is the natural juices of the vegetables that create the incredible flavour of this dish. It is most enjoyed by Greeks in the summertime, when vegetables are at their most magical. However, it also makes a terrific winter warmer. Traditionally, you cut the vegetables into quarters and cook in a roasting tray but I love the way I've done it here, as it shows off the beautiful colours of the vegetables and celebrates that good food can be simple when cooked with love.

Preheat the oven to 180°C (360°F).

Mix 170 ml (5½ fl oz/⅔ cup) of the olive oil with tomatoes, tomato paste, garlic, potato, half the Greek oregano, paprika, mint, onion, eggplant, capsicum and zucchini in a large bowl and season with salt and pepper. Set aside to marinate for at least 30 minutes to allow all the flavours to blend with the vegetables.

Grease an about 30 cm (12 in) round tray with 4 tablespoons of the extra-virgin olive oil and layer vegetables snugly on the tray in a circular shape, alternating each vegetable to create a colourful contrast.

Pour over the water, drizzle with remaining olive oil and sprinkle with remaining Greek oregano and rosemary. Pour over any juices remaining in the bowl. Bake for 2 hours, or until golden brown. Season to taste, and serve.

MAKE IT VEGAN

It already is!

MAKE IT GLUTEN-FREE

It already is!

WHAT TO DO WITH LEFTOVERS

Grease a frying pan over a medium heat with oil, lay leftover sliced vegetables over the base and pour over a few beaten eggs. Crumble over your favourite Greek cheese and fresh herbs and cook for 2–3 minutes each side, flipping once, to make a delicious omelette.

Γεμιστά

Yemista | Stuffed vegetables

SERVES 4

8 large ripe tomatoes
3 capsicums (bell peppers),
   in mixed colours
2 zucchinis (courgettes)
2 eggplants (aubergines)
1 teaspoon sugar
120 ml (4 fl oz) extra-virgin
   olive oil
2 onions, finely sliced
3 spring onions (scallions),
   sliced
4 garlic cloves, finely diced
60 ml (2 fl oz/¼ cup) tinned
   crushed tomatoes
125 ml (4 fl oz/½ cup) water
1 tablespoon pine nuts
60 g (2 oz/½ cup) sultanas
20 g (¾ oz/½ cup) each of
   mint, parsley and basil
200 g (7 oz/1 cup) long-grain
   rice
1 teaspoon sweet paprika
1 teaspoon dried Greek
   oregano
4 large potatoes, cut into
   wedges
salt and pepper, to taste
Greek feta or yoghurt, to
   serve

My mum, Sia, first learnt how to make yemista from her beloved aunt when she was just six years old. The first time she made it, she burnt it, just like I did my first time. This is a dish that may take a few times to get just right, so it's one to save for an afternoon when you have a bit of time. The effort is worth it – this dish is like a long, warm embrace that just makes you feel good. It is a lathera dish, which means it's cooked with an olive oil base (ladi means olive oil in Greek). This was a dish that became popular in post-war Greece with Greeks who had escaped from Turkey.

Cut the top off each tomato like you are giving it a bowl haircut. Try not to separate it from the rest of the tomato, so it sits like a lid on top.

Next, using a small spoon, gently scoop out the insides of the tomato without breaking its outer shell.

Place the scooped-out flesh in a bowl, grating any chunky pieces, and set aside.

Slice top and stem off capsicums, reserving the tops, and use a small sharp knife to remove the pith and seeds. Slice one end off the zucchinis and use a long teaspoon and a small paring knife to scoop out the flesh, being careful not to puncture the skin. Add to the tomato flesh in the bowl.

Slice the top off each eggplant (do it with care, as you will need to replace the lid once the eggplant is stuffed) and, using a spoon or a knife, carve the flesh out of the eggplants, leaving at least ½ cm (¼ inch) of wall intact. Add the flesh to the tomato and zucchini mixture, grating all pieces.

Place all the hollowed vegetables in a greased roasting tin and put a pinch of sugar at the bottom of each one, which will help sweeten them.

Heat 3 tablespoons of the extra-virgin olive oil in a frying pan over a low heat. Add the onion, spring onion and garlic and cook gently for 5 minutes, or until softened. Add the rice and cook for 5 minutes.

Recipe continues →

Add reserved vegetable flesh, tinned tomatoes and 125 ml (4 fl oz/½ cup) water. Season with salt and pepper and cook for a further 5 minutes.

Add the pine nuts, sultanas and herbs. Cook, stirring, for a further minute, then remove from the heat.

Preheat the oven to 180°C (360°F).

Gently scoop the cooked vegetable mixture into each hollowed vegetable, filling each to about three-quarters full (take care not to overfill, because the rice mixture will expand during cooking). Close the lids of each tomato and replace lids on capsicums and eggplants.

You will usually find your bowl with a little leftover tomato, rice and vegetable mixture. Pour it all over the top of the stuffed vegetables, grating any larger chunks, and drizzle with 3 tablespoons of olive oil.

Pour remaining water into the base of the roasting tin so the vegetables don't burn while baking.

Season with salt and pepper to taste and sprinkle with paprika and Greek oregano.

Place a wedge of potato between each vegetable to help keep them in place and add a little texture.

Cover with foil and bake for 30 minutes, then remove foil and bake for a further 60 minutes until deep golden brown. Once golden brown with some dark colour as pictured (don't be afraid of this, you really want the vegetables cooked well), you can serve with some Greek feta or yoghurt on top.

Kali orexi!

MAKE IT VEGAN

It already is! If using feta or yoghurt, you can use vegan feta or a Greek-style soy, plant-based or coconut yoghurt.

MAKE IT GLUTEN-FREE

It already is!

WHAT TO DO WITH LEFTOVERS

With any leftover rice filling, make fried rice patties. Place leftover rice filling in a bowl, add some breadcrumbs and a couple of beaten eggs and mix to combine. Shape into patties, roll in flour and fry until golden.

Γεμιστά κρεμμύδια

Onion yemista

SERVES 4

8 large onions
120 ml (4 fl oz) extra-virgin
   olive oil
extra 2 onions, finely sliced
1 teaspoon sugar
3 spring onions (scallions),
   sliced
4 garlic cloves, finely diced
200 g (7 oz/1 cup) long-grain
   rice
60 ml (2 fl oz/¼ cup) tinned
   crushed tomatoes
125 ml (4 fl oz/½ cup) water
salt and pepper, to taste
1 tablespoon pine nuts
60 g (2 oz/½ cup) sultanas
20 g (¾ oz/½ cup) each mint,
   parsley and basil
1 teaspoon sweet paprika
1 teaspoon dried
   Greek oregano
4 large potatoes, cut
   into wedges
1 tablespoon finely
   chopped dill
Greek feta or yoghurt,
   to serve

MAKE IT VEGAN
   It already is!

MAKE IT GLUTEN-FREE
   It already is!

WHAT TO DO WITH LEFTOVERS
   Take the leftover rice mix and mix
   with eggs, breadcrumbs and flour
   and fry into rice patties or reheat the
   rice mix and enjoy with some fried
   green beans.

We rarely think of stuffing onions but they truly are such a delightful surprise. You can make them as a standalone dish or mix them in with the rest of a traditional yemista roasting tray of vegetables with tomatoes, eggplant (aubergine) and zucchini (courgette).

Peel the outer skin of the onions and cut each onion through the middle, halfway down. Bring a large saucepan of water to the boil, add onions and cook for 10 minutes. Drain and set aside to cool.

Heat 3 tablespoons of the extra-virgin olive oil in a frying pan over a low heat. Add the extra sliced onions, sugar, spring onion and garlic and cook gently for 5 minutes, or until softened. Add the rice and cook for 5 minutes.

Add tinned tomatoes and the water. Season with salt and pepper and cook for a further 5 minutes.

Add the pine nuts, sultanas and herbs. Cook, stirring, for a further minute, then remove from the heat.

Cut the rest of the way down through each onion (you will notice each layer of onion will now come off like little lasagne sheets). Each onion will create about 5 onion sheets. Set aside. Now place 1 teaspoon of mixture in each onion sheet and then close them back up like a cocoon.

Place a large pot over a medium heat and brush with olive oil. Place stuffed onions and wedges in the bottom of the pot, layering snugly. Pour in just enough water to cover and season with salt and pepper. Cover with a plate or lid and cook for 10 minutes until mixture starts to boil, then remove lid and continue to cook for another 15–20 minutes, or until water is absorbed. Serve with dill and feta.

κρεμμύδι στιφάδο σε πουρέ πατάτας

Onion stifado on mashed potatoes

SERVES 4

8 small potatoes
50 g (1¾ oz) butter
1 teaspoon freshly grated
    nutmeg
salt and pepper, to taste
15 g (½ oz/¼ cup) flat-leaf
    (Italian) parsley, finely
    chopped
15 g (½ oz/¼ cup) chives,
    finely chopped
200 g (7 oz/2 cups)
    kefalograviera cheese,
    coarsely grated
1 tablespoon extra-virgin
    olive oil
125 ml (4 fl oz/½ cup) milk

Stifado is traditionally a very slowly cooked casserole made with rabbit, beef or octopus and small pearl onions in a rich red wine sauce with spices and herbs. The word stifado originates from the Ancient Greek word tyfos and its roots in Greece are found in the 13th century when the Venetians introduced it to the areas they had invaded and occupied.

Here I wanted to provide a vegetarian version of this dish, so we left out the meat and instead created a gorgeous Greek mashed potato to go with the shallot onions. Then we slowly cook our red wine, spice and herb sauce to make this an equally hearty and comforting meal for any season.

Bring a large saucepan of water to the boil. Add the potatoes and cook for 15–20 minutes, or until tender but not mushy (you can test if they are ready by poking a knife into the potatoes to see if it easily goes into the centre without falling apart). Drain and transfer potatoes to a bowl. Mash with a potato masher or fork.

Add the butter, nutmeg, salt and pepper, herbs, cheese and olive oil. Gradually pour in milk, mixing as you go with a wooden spoon, until you reach your desired consistency.

Now find an oval serving dish and spread the mash over with a spoon in preparation for layering the onion stifado on top.

TO MAKE THE ONION STIFADO

Make 4 small slits around each onion, cutting into the first couple of layers of the onion (this will help them cook more easily).

Heat extra-virgin olive oil in a large pot over a low heat and add the onions. Cover the pot with the lid and cook for 10 minutes, gently shaking the pot regularly using its handles (do not stir the onions with a spoon as we want to keep them intact).

After 10 minutes the onions should be starting to get some colour. Add the garlic and cook for a couple of minutes, then add the red wine or white vinegar and cook for a further couple of minutes until it reduces completely. Add the rosemary,

ONION STIFADO

1 kg (2 lb 3 oz) French
   shallots, peeled
80 ml (2½ fl oz/⅓ cup)
   extra-virgin olive oil
3 garlic cloves, finely diced
125 ml (4 fl oz/½ cup) red
   wine (shiraz, pinot or
   cabernet merlot) or 80 ml
   (2½ fl oz/⅓ cup) white
   vinegar
1 tablespoon roughly
   chopped rosemary
1 cinnamon stick
2 cloves
2 bay leaves
salt and pepper, to taste
1 tablespoon tomato paste
200 g (7 oz) tinned crushed
   tomatoes
1 teaspoon vegetable stock
   powder

cinnamon, cloves and bay leaves, cook for a further 2 minutes and season with salt and pepper. Rather than stirring the pot, keep mixing it by gently shaking the pot from the handles.

Add the tomato paste, tinned tomato, vegetable stock powder and enough water to almost fully cover the onions. Bring to the boil, then reduce to a simmer and cook for 5–7 minutes, or until cooking liquids are almost evaporated.

Spoon onion stifado over the mashed potato to serve.

MAKE IT VEGAN
   It already is!

MAKE IT GLUTEN-FREE
   It already is!

WHAT TO DO WITH LEFTOVERS
   Wrap this dish with foil and
   refrigerate and it will be just as
   wonderful the next day with some
   kefalograviera, kasseri or manouri
   cheese grated over it.

Ψητά λαχανικά σε ελληνική μαρινάδα

Marinated grilled vegetable platter

SERVES 8

2 eggplants (aubergines),
   thinly sliced
2 zucchinis (courgettes),
   thinly sliced
2 red capsicums (bell
   peppers), thickly sliced
400 g asparagus (about
   2 bunches)
250 g (9 oz) mushrooms
250 g (9 oz) cherry tomatoes
freshly chopped parsley,
   to serve

MARINADE
375 ml (12½ fl oz/1½ cups)
   extra-virgin olive oil
4 garlic cloves, diced
1 teaspoon dill seeds
1 tablespoon sherry vinegar
2 teaspoons white vinegar
1 teaspoon Greek oregano
1 sprig fresh rosemary, leaves
   picked
1 sprig fresh lemon thyme,
   leaves picked
salt and pepper, to taste

You do not need to spend a small fortune at your local deli to enjoy delicious grilled vegetables such as eggplant (aubergine), zucchini (courgette), mushrooms, capsicums (bell peppers), cherry tomatoes and asparagus.

Preheat the oven to 180°C (360°F) or preheat the barbecue grill to high.

To make the marinade, combine olive oil, garlic, dill seeds, sherry vinegar, white vinegar, Greek oregano, rosemary, lemon thyme and salt and pepper in a large bowl. Add vegetables and toss to combine. Leave the vegetables to marinate for an hour in the fridge before roasting.

If you are using an oven, place eggplant, zucchini and capsicum in a roasting tin with the leftover marinade juices and cook for 20 minutes. Add the asparagus, mushrooms and cherry tomatoes and cook for a further 15–20 minutes, or until vegetables are golden brown.

If you are using a barbecue, grill the vegetables. These vegetables take different times to grill so add them at different times. The capsicum will take about 15 minutes, the eggplant and zucchini 8–10 minutes, the asparagus, cherry tomatoes and mushrooms about 5 minutes (ensure you turn them halfway through cooking so they cook evenly).

Top with a handful of freshly chopped parsley to serve.

MAKE IT VEGAN

It already is!

MAKE IT GLUTEN-FREE

It already is!

WHAT TO DO WITH LEFTOVERS

These barbecued vegetables make for a terrific pizza topping or use them as part of the filling for a moussaka.

Πατάτες Λεμονάτες

Patates lemonates | Roasted lemon potatoes

SERVES 6

6 large potatoes
1 teaspoon finely chopped
    lemon thyme leaves
2 teaspoons finely chopped
    rosemary leaves
1 teaspoon dried Greek
    oregano
juice of 1 large lemon
1 teaspoon vegetable stock
salt and pepper, to taste
250 ml (8½ fl oz/1 cup) water
125 ml (4 fl oz/½ cup)
    extra-virgin olive oil

There is something disarmingly special about Greek potatoes. You may be asking, how good can they be if they are just potatoes? But it is not until you take your first bite of the lemon, olive oil and herb goodness that you truly appreciate how special these are. This is a dish cooked slowly with a very generous amount of olive oil, which people may think is over the top. However, that olive oil is good for you, and you get to dip your bread into it as an extra treat. This dish can also be made by cutting the potatoes into wedges and using the same marinade – they are just as delicious.

Preheat the oven to 200°C (390°F).

Peel, wash and slice the potatoes into about 5 mm (¼ in) thick slices using a knife or mandoline.

Combine all the ingredients (except the water and olive oil) in a large bowl and gently toss together. Arrange potato slices stacked up against each other like dominoes in a large roasting tin (don't pack them too tightly as they need room to breathe and cook). Pour the water into the base of the tin and drizzle extra-virgin olive oil all over the potatoes. Cook for about 1 hour and 30 minutes, or until golden and crisp.

MAKE IT VEGAN

It already is!

MAKE IT GLUTEN-FREE

It already is!

WHAT TO DO WITH LEFTOVERS

You can blend any leftover potatoes into a delicious lemon herb mash. As for the juices – they are divine dipped into toasted bread or mixed with a tin of cannellini beans and then fried or baked to create lovely lemon-infused beans.

HOPE

I founded my charity, the Asylum Seeker Resource Centre, when I was 28. It is now the largest independent organisation in Australia helping refugees and people seeking asylum. The centre was born out of my recognition of the importance of food justice and security, prompted by the struggles of my grandparents and parents. And from my understanding that I have simply won the lottery when it comes to being in the right place at the right time and, in another situation, it could so easily be me needing help.

People seeking asylum were going hungry in my local community, denied the right to an income, health care or a safety net. I asked myself, how can you find sanctuary and safety and sustain yourself for the journey to freedom if you are hungry? How can a prosperous country call itself civilised when it denies those seeking protection the basic succour needed to survive?
So I decided to do something about it.

I was teaching 40 TAFE students at the time and, as part of a class project, we started a food bank. There were some amazing, passionate students, such as Sherrine, with whom I have remained friends to this day. Created in eight weeks in a tiny shopfront in the working class suburb of Footscray in Melbourne, with the support of my sister, Nola, my mum, Sia, and friends Pablo and Diana, it sought to provide food security to families who were left to perish in my city.

These were families who had the courage to split the earth in half to save their children. They had bravely survived the horrors of war, the treachery of people smugglers and

Be kind, for everyone you meet is fighting a hard battle.

– **PLATO**

unforgiving seas that sought to engulf their hope, only to then be punished by my country for not drowning at sea.

The wicked plan of John Howard's government at the time was to starve refugees of hope by seeking to erase their ability to be seen, to survive, to feed their families or contribute to their community. The thinking was that left with no food, income, health care or the right to even work, refugees would give up and return to the arms of their torturers and oppressors. The Australian Government was banking on no one helping these refugees.

We would make sure that every family that came into our food bank for help would know they would be welcomed, seen and cared for. The simple act of providing food for their families gave refugees not just a sense of relief from hunger but a sense of belonging and hope.

Soon after, I started cooking meals in our humble kitchen. I could only afford a gas burner used for camping in our first kitchen but we found a way to start cooking meals for dozens of people.

Each day, we would sit together and share a meal. In those moments we were like a big, extended family, sharing a meal of welcome and seeing our shared humanity. The sharing of a meal and the act of hospitality that is at the heart of this is universal to refugees.

I have had refugee families invite me to their homes to say thank you for winning them asylum and we would be sitting on the floor because they could not afford any furniture. In front of me on a blanket would be the most incredible feast drawn from their culture. Whatever food and means they had was in that meal, to show not just gratitude but that no one can rob them of their welcome, their generosity, their dignity, their culture.

I remember being on Manus Island, an offshore detention centre where refugees were being held, where I had been smuggled in to document the human rights abuses happening there. There I was in the middle of the night, in a prison where the Australian Government had cut off water, food and electricity and the first thing the refugees, who had been locked up there for five years, did was make us a cup of tea and share what biscuits they had. For these men, being able to welcome us as they would at home, was an act of resistance and defiance. It was the most profound message – 'We are still here, we will not be robbed of our humanity even if you have lost yours.'

Sharing a daily meal together is now a 20-year-old (and counting!) tradition at the ASRC. It is a ritual of hope that, no matter how dark the day may be when it begins, there is a place where you are welcome. Here languages from across the globe are spoken, laughter and smiles rise up and, even when a language is not shared, there is a shared story. Sharing a meal gives us this gift.

I can be sharing a beautiful meal at my work at the ASRC with refugees from 60 countries, faiths, religions or languages, and we all understand each other. No words need be spoken, we see each other and our shared humanity. Imagine if we could see each other like this every day, part of one big family, all deserving to be seen, and feel safe and loved. There is an adage we need to remember: we do not need tougher borders or higher walls, we need longer tables where everyone can have a seat.

Μπάμιες

Stovetop okra

SERVES 4

1 kg (2 lb 3 oz) okra
80 ml (2½ fl oz/⅓ cup) white
    vinegar
1 teaspoon salt
80 ml (2½ fl oz/⅓ cup)
    extra-virgin olive oil
2 onions, diced
2 garlic cloves, crushed
1 tablespoon tomato paste
400 g (14 oz) tinned tomatoes
    or 3 tomatoes, peeled
    and grated
1 teaspoon sugar
salt and pepper, to taste
50 g (1¾ oz) Greek feta,
    to serve

While the origin of okra is debated – although it is most likely that it came from somewhere near Ethiopia – what is beyond dispute is that it is as much loved in Greek cooking as it is in African cooking. Often people are turned off by okra because of its stickiness when cooking it. Soaking the okra in white vinegar overnight before cooking helps address this.

Cut the rough edges from the stem of the okra; be careful not to cut so deep that you release its juices. Mix the okra, vinegar and salt in a bowl, toss to combine and set aside for 30 minutes. Drain and rinse.

Heat half the oil in a large saucepan over a medium heat and sauté the onion and garlic until softened. Add the tomato paste, tomatoes and sugar. Season with salt and pepper. Add the okra (if using fresh tomatoes, also add 125 ml/4 fl oz/½ cup of water at this time). Drizzle with the remaining extra-virgin olive oil.

Cook for 25 minutes without stirring, shaking the pan occasionally, until most of the liquid has evaporated, then reduce heat to low and cook for a further 5 minutes, then remove from the heat. Crumble feta over to serve.

MAKE IT VEGAN

It already is!

MAKE IT GLUTEN-FREE

It already is!

WHAT TO DO WITH LEFTOVERS

You can repurpose the okra in so many different dishes. Fry up some onions and garlic, add any other vegetables you desire, such as zucchini (courgette), potatoes or green beans, and toss in the leftover okra. Finish with crumbled Greek feta to serve.

Μελιτζάνα καπαμά

Eggplant kapama

SERVES 6

4 Lebanese eggplants (aubergines), peeled and chopped into large chunks
1 tablespoon salt
125 ml (4 fl oz/½ cup) extra-virgin olive oil
4 large onions, quartered
5 garlic cloves, diced
15 g (½ oz/½ cup) flat-leaf (Italian) parsley, chopped
15 g (½ oz/¼ cup) basil, chopped
5 g (⅛ oz/ ¼ cup) mint, chopped
200 g (7 oz) tinned diced tomatoes
1 tablespoon tomato paste
1 teaspoon vegetable stock powder
1 teaspoon cinnamon
1 teaspoon freshly grated nutmeg
400 ml (13½ fl oz) water
salt and pepper, to taste

Kapama, in Greek cooking, means dishes that are slowly braised in a tomato sauce – our favourite vegetables to cook using this method are cauliflower, okra, long flat beans and potatoes. The magic of this dish is in allowing the eggplant (aubergine) to slowly take in the juices and flavours of the tomato, oil and herbs. The key is to trust it to soften while cooking and not to stir it around continuously; rather, gently shake the pot using the handles, to make sure it fully cooks and absorbs its sauce to achieve an irresistible 'melt in the mouth' texture.

Like many Greek dishes, it also has lots of fresh herbs. Greek herbs are central to our cooking, with our most popular herbs being those we have been using for thousands of years, from Greek oregano (rigani), dill (anthos), mint (menta), sideritis, basil (vassilikos) and Greek mountain tea (tsai tou vounou).

Historically, herbs were believed to have a range of powers, from the medicinal to the superstitious. Greek oregano was planted to ward off evil spirits and basil hung on doors to bring good luck.

Place eggplant in a bowl, add salt and cover with water. Set aside for 30 minutes, then drain.

Heat oil in a large saucepan over a low heat and sauté onion and garlic until softened. Add eggplant and keep cooking on low heat until the eggplant softens. Add herbs and stir through, then add tinned tomatoes and tomato paste, vegetable stock powder, cinnamon, nutmeg, water and season with salt and pepper. Cook for 30–40 minutes, or until the sauce thickens and the eggplant is very soft.

MAKE IT VEGAN
It already is!

MAKE IT GLUTEN-FREE
It already is!

WHAT TO DO WITH LEFTOVERS
The leftovers would make a terrific sauce to toss your favourite pasta through.

Αγκινάρες αλα πολίτα

Greek artichoke and broad bean fricassee

SERVES 4

80 ml (2½ fl oz/⅓ cup) extra-virgin olive oil, plus extra for drizzling
3 onions, finely diced
2 celery sticks, chopped
3 small potatoes, halved
1 spring onion (scallion), sliced
2 small carrots, sliced
1 fennel bulb, finely sliced
15 g (1 oz/½ cup) flat-leaf (Italian) parsley, chopped
30 g (1 oz/½ cup) dill, chopped
10 g (1 oz/½ cup) mint, chopped
250 g (9 oz) fresh or frozen broad beans
½ head lettuce, roughly chopped
1 teaspoon sweet paprika
salt and pepper, to taste
250 g (9 oz) (about 6) artichokes (fresh, bottled or tinned), halved
2 eggs
juice of 3 lemons
1 tablespoon plain (all-purpose) flour
1 teaspoon water
1 teaspoon freshly chopped dill, to serve

MAKE IT VEGAN
Replace the eggs with a vegan egg mix or leave out.

MAKE IT GLUTEN-FREE
It already is!

WHAT TO DO WITH LEFTOVERS
Place leftovers in a bowl, cover well with plastic wrap and refrigerate. Reheat on the stovetop on low heat the next day to enjoy again.

Fricassee is a classic French cooking method that produces something between a sautéed dish and a stew. It has been adopted by the Greeks, showcasing again how Greek cuisine has been influenced by other food cultures for thousands of years. In Greek cuisine the most popular dish using this method has traditionally been lamb fricassee with an avgolemono (egg and lemon) sauce (unlike French cuisine, which uses a cream sauce). It also makes a delicious soup that is often enjoyed at Easter.

Heat the oil in a large pot over a low heat and sauté the onion for 2 minutes. Add the celery and fry for a further 3 minutes, then add the potato and fry for another 3 minutes.

Add the spring onion, carrot, fennel and herbs and cook for another 5 minutes. Add the broad beans and lettuce and cook for a further 5 minutes.

Add the sweet paprika and season with salt and pepper. Add enough water to cover all the ingredients, bring to the boil, then reduce to a simmer and cook for 15 minutes.

Add the artichokes and gently push them under the juices. Cook for another 5 minutes until little of the juices is left and the potatoes are tender. Remove from the heat and set aside.

Place the eggs in a small bowl and beat well. Add the lemon juice and beat again. In a separate small bowl, combine the flour and water to form a paste. Gradually stir in the egg mixture. Pour the mixture all over the fricassee and set aside for 5 minutes. Drizzle with extra oil and sprinkle with dill to serve.

———

KON'S TIP: *If you are using fresh artichokes, you can use a slightly different approach. Firstly clean the artichokes and halve and place in a bowl of cold water and lemon juice to ensure they do not discolour. Place in a small pot of boiling water and cook for 5 minutes, then drain.*

Κουνουπίδι καπαμά

Kounoupidi kapama | Braised cauliflower

SERVES 6

canola oil, for deep-frying
2 large cauliflower, divided
    into large florets
4 potatoes, quartered
200 ml (7 fl oz) water
salt and pepper, to taste
Greek feta, to serve
extra-virgin olive oil, for drizzling

TOMATO SAUCE
80 ml (2½ fl oz/⅓ cup)
    extra-virgin olive oil
2 onions, quartered
1 teaspoon sugar
2 garlic cloves
400 g (14 oz) tinned crushed
    tomatoes
1 tablespoon tomato paste
1 bay leaf
1 teaspoon sweet paprika
3 cloves
15 g (½ oz/½ cup) flat-leaf
    (Italian) parsley, finely
    chopped
salt and pepper, to taste
10 g (¼ oz/½ cup) mint, finely
    chopped

MAKE IT VEGAN

It already is!

MAKE IT GLUTEN-FREE

It already is!

WHAT TO DO WITH LEFTOVERS

Take 3 cans of butter beans, drain, wash and toss them into a roasting pan. Pour all the leftover juices and cauliflower over them. Gently shake the tray, add some more extra-virgin olive oil and salt and pepper and then bake for about 45 minutes at 180°C (360°F) and you will have a hearty variation on the Greek favourite, Gigantes (page 164).

I find the most humble of recipes can be the most pleasurable, and this dish is no exception. It allows the cauliflower to be the rightful hero of the dish, roasted slowly in a fragrant, herbed tomato sauce. You can cook it on its own or with potatoes, green beans or zucchinis to enjoy its beautiful sauce and, if in the mood, finish it with some Greek feta and more extra-virgin olive oil.

Half-fill a large frying pan with canola oil over a medium heat and wait until the oil is very hot. Add cauliflower in batches, frying each batch until golden, taking care not to burn or overcrowd the wok, as it won't cook them properly. Gently turn the cauliflower with a fork to get colour on all sides. Add a few pinches of salt to the cauliflower while it is frying. Once golden, remove from the oil, using a slotted spoon, and set aside on a paper towel to drain.

Return the pan with the residual oil to a medium heat and heat again until hot. Add potatoes in batches and cook until golden, transferring to a paper towel to drain. The key is to nicely fry the potatoes and cauliflower but not cook them through – they will cook fully in the oven.

Grease a 3 litre (101 fl oz/12 cup) ovenproof roasting tin with oil. Add cooked cauliflower and potato to the tin.

Now it is time to make the simple Greek tomato sauce that will cover these gorgeous vegetables.

Heat the olive oil in a frying pan over a low heat. Sauté onion until softened and golden. Add sugar and stir to combine to give the onion some sweetness. Add garlic, tinned tomatoes, tomato paste, bay leaf, paprika, cloves, parsley and mint and season with salt and pepper. Cook for 15 minutes, then pour over the cauliflower and potato in the roasting tin and mix with your hands to make sure they are fully covered.

Preheat the oven to 200°C (390°F). Add water to prevent the cauliflower and potato from sticking or burning, season with salt and pepper and drizzle with extra-virgin olive oil. Roast for 1 hour or until the vegetables are dark and golden and the juices are reduced but the oil remains (as is the Greek way when making a lathera dish 'in the oil'). Crumble over feta and drizzle with extra oil to serve.

Γίγαντες

Gigantes | Baked 'giant' beans

SERVES 6

500 g (1 lb 2 oz) butter (lima)
    beans
80 ml (2½ fl oz/⅓ cup)
    extra-virgin olive oil
1 onion, diced
1 teaspoon sugar
3 garlic cloves, finely chopped
3 small carrot roughly diced
1 stalk celery, roughly diced
400 g (14 oz) tinned crushed
    tomatoes
3 cloves
400 ml (13½ fl oz) water
½ teaspoon freshly grated
    nutmeg
½ teaspoon sweet paprika
1 tablespoon tomato paste
salt and pepper, to taste
2 tablespoons breadcrumbs
1 tablespoon roughly
    chopped basil
1 tablespoon roughly
    chopped parsley
1 tablespoon roughly
    chopped mint
2 tomatoes, sliced (optional)

I love the versatility of this dish – Greek baked beans in a rich tomato sauce that you can enjoy any time of day. At breakfast, you can scoop some of the leftovers onto some thick toast, drizzle with a little extra-virgin olive oil and crumble some feta on it. Or, at lunch time, you can enjoy it as a main dish with a side of feta and olives.

Bring a large pot of water to the boil, add the beans and cook for 30 minutes, then drain and set aside.

Heat extra-virgin olive oil in the same pot over a low heat. Sauté onion and sugar for a few minutes, then add garlic and cook until softened. Add carrot and celery and sauté for a further 5 minutes until softened. Add tinned tomatoes, cloves and water.

Add the nutmeg, paprika, tomato paste and season with salt and pepper.

Bring to the boil then reduce to a low heat to simmer for about 15 minutes, or until thickened. Add fresh herbs and cook for a further 5 minutes. Add beans and toss to combine.

Preheat the oven to 180°C (360°F). Transfer mixture to a roasting tin and cover with sliced tomatoes (these are optional and can be left out if you like). Sprinkle with the breadcrumbs and bake for about 30 minutes, or until golden.

MAKE IT VEGAN

It already is!

MAKE IT GLUTEN-FREE

Use gluten-free breadcrumbs.

WHAT TO DO WITH LEFTOVERS

Gigantes taste even better the day after. They're great on toasted bread, sprinkled with herbs and extra-virgin olive oil.

Πατάτες με χτένια

Scalloped potatoes

SERVES 8

6 large potatoes, thinly sliced
3 garlic cloves, grated
pepper, to taste
1 tablespoon vegetable stock
   powder
1 teaspoon salt
1 small onion, thinly sliced
1 teaspoon extra-virgin
   olive oil
250 ml (8½ fl oz/1 cup)
   pouring cream

This dish is one of my mum's favourite dishes to make and eat at Easter time. Sia always makes it with such pride and I understand why – it's just divine. It is the first dish my mum tries to convince everyone to try, and when I mention it is hard to go wrong with cream and potatoes, my mum gives me the saltiest of looks! The mix of cream, garlic and onions gives it this lovely flavour and it is so rich and tasty.

Preheat the oven to 180°C (360°F). Place potatoes in a large bowl. Add garlic, pepper, vegetable stock powder, salt, onion and olive oil and toss to combine. Arrange potatoes in layers in a roasting tin and pour over cream. Bake for 50 minutes, or until golden.

MAKE IT VEGAN

By using a vegan cream.

MAKE IT GLUTEN-FREE

It already is!

WHAT TO DO WITH LEFTOVERS

You could put the leftovers in a blender, add some fresh chopped herbs and make a delicious creamy mash potatoes.

Λαδερά λαχανικά

Lathera vegetables

SERVES 6

2 tablespoons extra-virgin
  olive oil, plus extra
  (optional) for drizzling
1 large onion, diced
250 g (9 oz) green beans,
  trimmed
4 potatoes, quartered
2 green capsicums
  (bell peppers)
2 eggplants (aubergines)
2 zucchinis (courgettes)
salt and pepper, to taste
420 g (15 oz) tinned chopped
  tomatoes
1 teaspoon tomato paste
250 ml (8½ fl oz/1 cup) water
15 g (½ oz/½ cup) flat-leaf
  (Italian) parsley, chopped
10 g (¼ oz/½ cup) fresh mint,
  chopped
Greek feta, crumbled, to
  serve (optional)

This recipe is part of the lathera family of recipes. In Greek, lathera means 'in oil' and when we say 'in oil', as Greeks, we are not messing around. These are usually vegetarian and vegan recipes cooked in significant amounts of extra-virgin olive oil, just like briam, fasolakia, horta and lemon potatoes, and finished with Greek feta and lots of bread.

The reason our diet is the healthiest in the world is that olive oil, 'the great healer' as Hippocrates called it, is at its heart. It's what we use for dressing and cooking almost everything we eat. Greek extra-virgin olive oil is packed with essential vitamins, full of calcium, iron, sodium and potassium and has the lowest acidity of any olive oil. It can reduce blood pressure and cholesterol and has anti-inflammatory benefits.

Heat olive oil in a large pot over a low heat. Cook onion for a few minutes until golden. Add beans and cook for 5 minutes. Add potatoes and cook for 2 minutes, then add capsicum and cook for a further 2 minutes. Add eggplant and zucchini, season well with salt and pepper, and cook for a further few minutes.

Add tinned tomatoes, tomato paste and water, season again and cook for a further 20 minutes. Add herbs and cook for a further 10 minutes. Set aside to cool slightly before serving. You can serve with crumbled feta and an extra drizzle of olive oil, if you like.

MAKE IT VEGAN

It already is!

MAKE IT GLUTEN-FREE

It already is!

WHAT TO DO WITH LEFTOVERS

Eat on toasted bread with feta or ricotta or bake in a roasting tray with your favourite canned beans tossed through to make a delicious baked bean casserole.

Ελληνικά χόρτα BBQ

Barbecued greens

SERVES 4

125 ml (4 fl oz/½ cup) extra-virgin olive oil
4 garlic cloves
salt and pepper, to taste
zest of 1 lemon
sprig of thyme
1 teaspoon Greek oregano
2 sprigs rosemary, leaves picked
1 bay leaf
250 g silverbeet (Swiss chard), rapini or chicory
100 g (3½ oz) Greek feta

We do not typically think about grilling greens like silverbeet (Swiss chard), chicory or rapini on a barbecue, but I am here to tell you, they taste amazing. Pick any greens you love, create your marinade and, as they are barbecuing, remember just to keep adding as much marinade as you like. You can finish them with fresh lemon, crumbled feta, fried halloumi and fresh ricotta.

Preheat the barbecue to hot.

Combine oil, garlic, salt, pepper, lemon zest, thyme, Greek oregano, rosemary and the bay leaf in a bowl.

Brush the barbecue grill or hotplate with some of the marinade mixture. Add greens, cover generously with the marinade and cook for a couple of minutes, then turn and cook for another couple of minutes until cooked.

Place on a large serving platter, pour over the remaining marinade, crumble Greek feta on top and serve.

MAKE IT VEGAN

By using a vegan feta or leave the feta out.

MAKE IT GLUTEN-FREE

It already is!

WHAT TO DO WITH LEFTOVERS

Roughly chop leftovers and add to a frying pan over a medium heat with some olive oil. Pour over some beaten eggs and top with your favourite grated cheese for a delicious omelette. They'd also make a great filling for a variation on batzina.

Αγκινάρες με λεμόνι, ελαιόλαδο και μυζήθρα

Artichokes in lemon, olive oil and mizithra

MEZZE DISH

6 fresh artichoke hearts
juice of 1 lemon
pinch of salt
80 ml (2½ fl oz) extra-virgin
   olive oil
50 g (1¾ oz) mizithra, grated

Cleaning artichokes is like an act of love; it takes patience, care and commitment, but it's worth it – they taste so much better fresh. Now, you need to be prepared for the fact that you start with these large magnificent artichokes and then end up with this mini version of them at the end, but sometimes less is more. When you clean the artichokes, you want to get all the leaves off, cut the hard parts of the stem off and clear all the inner fluff so you are left with just the heart itself, then place them in water with squeezed lemon to make sure they don't darken while waiting to cook. Quick tip: if the stem of a fresh artichoke is hard and won't bend, it means the artichoke is no good – you want a stem that is soft.

Place the artichokes in a small pot of water and bring to the boil. Reduce heat to a simmer and cook for 10 minutes, or until tender. Place in a colander to dry.

Thinly slice the artichokes and transfer to a serving platter. Sprinkle with lemon juice and the pinch of salt, drizzle with olive oil and sprinkle with the mizithra.

MAKE IT VEGAN

Use a vegan mizithra or parmesan.

MAKE IT GLUTEN-FREE

It already is!

WHAT TO DO WITH LEFTOVERS

Make a delicious sandwich using this as the filling the next day.

Αγκινάρες και κουκιά σε πλούσια σάλτσα ντομάτας

Artichokes and broad beans in a rich tomato sauce

SERVES 4

3 tablespoons extra-virgin olive oil

1 onion, finely diced

1 teaspoon sugar

1 fennel bulb, roughly chopped

500 g (1 lb 2 oz) fresh broad beans in their skin (use only small, young ones), podded (or 300 g/10½ oz frozen podded beans)

10 g (1¼ oz/½ cup) mint, chopped

15 g (½ oz/½ cup) flat-leaf (Italian) parsley, chopped

30 g (1 oz/½ cup) dill, chopped

1 teaspoon sweet paprika

400 g (14 oz) tinned crushed tomatoes

1 tablespoon tomato paste

250 ml (8½ fl oz/1 cup) water

salt and pepper, to taste

250 g (6) artichokes (fresh, bottled or tinned), sliced in half

MAKE IT VEGAN

It already is!

MAKE IT GLUTEN-FREE

It already is!

WHAT TO DO WITH LEFTOVERS

Cook up your favourite rice the next day and serve the leftovers on top with a side of toasted pita bread and some Greek-style yoghurt or Greek feta to garnish.

The Ancient Greeks considered artichokes an aphrodisiac and claimed that consuming them would guarantee that a mother would give birth to a boy! Artichokes were also highly sought after to assist liver function and compensate for the excesses of eating and drinking, and they remain a modern-day superfood due to being so high in dietary fibre and antioxidants.

Heat oil in a frying pan over a low heat. Sauté onion and sugar for 2 minutes. Add fennel and gently fry for 2 minutes. If using fresh broad beans, boil them for 10 minutes. Add the broad beans to the pan and fry for 2 minutes.

Add herbs, gently stir through and fry for 2 minutes.

Add sweet paprika, tinned tomatoes, tomato paste and water and season with salt and pepper.

Bring to the boil and then reduce to simmer and cook for 20 minutes until sauce thickens. Carefully add the halved artichokes, spreading them around the pan and pushing them under the sauce, and cook for a further 10 minutes. You want a nice thick sauce. Remove from heat and set aside for 5 minutes before serving.

———

KON'S TIP: *If you are using fresh artichokes, you can use a slightly different approach. Firstly clean the artichokes and halve and place in a bowl of cold water and lemon juice to ensure they do not discolour. Place in a small pot of boiling water and cook for 5 minutes, then drain. Add the fresh artichokes at the same time as the tinned tomatoes rather than with 10 minutes to go.*

Pies, Pastries
& Breads

Μπατζίνα

Batzina | Zucchini pie

SERVES 6

4 zucchinis (courgettes),
  grated
1 teaspoon salt
4 tablespoons Greek-style
  yoghurt
3 eggs
2 spring onions (scallions),
  chopped
20 g (1¾ oz/1 cup) chopped
  mint
60 g (2 oz/1 cup) chopped dill
30 g (2 oz/1 cup) flat-leaf
  (Italian) chopped parsley
90 g (3 oz) plain (all-purpose)
  flour
1 tablespoon baking powder
200 g (7 oz) Greek feta,
  crumbled
salt and pepper, to taste
4 teaspoons extra-virgin
  olive oil
100 g (3½ oz) breadcrumbs

This is a delicious crustless savoury pie that originated in Thessaly. As it's pastry free, it's lovely and light. It is a versatile recipe as you can substitute the zucchini (courgette) for everything from grated pumpkin (winter squash) or sweet potato to any cheese, or even use the zucchini without the eggs and cheese. This is a dish that you can enjoy hot or cold. Note: it's not a thick Greek pie, rather it is crisp and thin, and it's lovely as a main or sliced into small slices as part of a mezze platter.

Put the grated zucchini in a colander, cover with salt and set aside to drain for 2 hours. Once drained, use your hands to squeeze out any remaining juice.

Preheat the oven to 180°C (360°F). Combine drained zucchini and all of the remaining ingredients (except for the oil and breadcrumbs) in a bowl, stirring gently with a wooden spoon to create a thick batter. Season with salt and pepper.

Grease a 30 cm (12 in) round cake tin with 2 teaspoons of olive oil and sprinkle 2 tablespoons of the breadcrumbs over the base of the tin (this will help reduce sticking). Pour mixture into tin and top with remaining breadcrumbs and olive oil. Bake for 40 minutes, or until golden.

MAKE IT VEGAN

Replace the eggs with a vegan egg mix or leave out altogether, use a vegan feta and substitute standard yoghurt with a Greek-style soy, plant-based or coconut yoghurt.

MAKE IT GLUTEN-FREE

Use gluten-free breadcrumbs and flour.

WHAT TO DO WITH LEFTOVERS

Batzina will comfortably last at least a week if stored in an airtight container in the fridge.

Σπανακόπιτα

Spanakopita | Spinach and feta pie

SERVES 8

DOUGH

1.6 kg (2 lb 3 oz) special white flour, farina flour or 00 plain flour, plus extra for dusting

2 tablespoons extra-virgin olive oil, plus extra for greasing

750 ml (25½ fl oz/3 cups) lukewarm water

1 tablespoon sugar

¼ teaspoon vinegar

½ teaspoon salt

50 g (1¾ oz) melted butter, for greasing

FILLING

250 g (9 oz) spinach, roughly chopped

250 g (9 oz) silverbeet (Swiss chard), roughly chopped

2 tablespoons salt

10 g (¼ oz/½ cup) mint, finely chopped

15 g (½ oz/½ cup) flat-leaf (Italian) parsley, finely chopped

30 g (1 oz/½ cup) dill, finely chopped

2 tablespoons extra-virgin olive oil

1 onion, finely diced

1 leek, finely chopped

1 bunch spring onions (scallions), finely chopped

250 g (9 oz) Greek feta

2 eggs, beaten

salt and pepper, to taste

The origins of one of the most beloved dishes in Greek cooking, spanakopita, dates back more than 400 years. The region of Epirus in the north-west of Greece is where the most renowned iterations of this dish come from. You will find this dish everywhere in Greece, from cafes and restaurants to bakeries and delis. The traditional way is to make your own phyllo pastry – this is a work of love, as it takes time and care but creates a texture and taste that store-bought phyllo just cannot replicate. However, you can definitely also use store-bought pastry in the same way if you prefer.

TO MAKE THE DOUGH

Place the flour into a large bowl and make a well. Add olive oil, water, sugar, vinegar and salt. Mix it together with your hands or with a wooden spoon.

Turn out the dough onto a lightly floured surface and knead for about 5 minutes until the dough is soft and it bounces back when you press into it with your fingers.

Place dough into a large oiled bowl, cover with plastic wrap and set aside in a warm place for 2 hours.

Meanwhile, prepare your filling.

Combine spinach, silverbeet, salt and herbs in a bowl and set aside for 2 hours (the salt will draw out the juices from the greens).

Heat olive oil in a frying pan over a low heat and fry the onion for 2 minutes. Add leek and fry for a further 5 minutes. Add spring onion and cook for a further 2 minutes.

Squeeze the spinach, silverbeet and herb mixture well and discard the juices (do not wash). Return to the bowl, add feta and egg and mix to combine, then stir in the cooked leek and onion mixture. Season with pepper and set aside.

GLAZE

1 egg yolk
1 teaspoon cold water

Preheat the oven to 180°C (360°F) and grease a 30 cm (12 in) square baking tray with melted butter.

Turn out the dough again onto a lightly floured surface and knead for a further 1–2 minutes until the dough is smooth. Divide into 8 equal-sized balls of dough.

Roll each into the size of a small pizza and place the dough into two piles of 4 doughs each, stacked on top of each other like pancakes.

Using a rolling pin, roll each stack of dough out into the widest and longest rectangular shape that you can to cover the size of your square 30 cm (12 in) baking tray. You will need to use your fingers to pull the edges of the phyllo dough gently to stretch out its size; be careful not to tear it. Place 1 layer of phyllo into the base of the baking tray.

Pour in the spinach and silverbeet mixture and spread evenly. Trim any phyllo overhanging the edges and fold any excess phyllo inwards to be covered by the next layer of phyllo.

Now add the second layer of phyllo and again cut the edges of the phyllo hanging over the tray. Using two fingers, gently push the top layer of phyllo down to ensure the mixture doesn't come out.

Using a sharp knife, cut the spanakopita into pieces of the size that you would like. It is critical to do this now before baking, as it will be too difficult to cut afterwards

Combine egg yolk and water to make a glaze, then brush the glaze all over the phyllo and edges.

Bake for about 1 hour, or until golden brown.

MAKE IT VEGAN

Use a vegan feta and leave eggs out altogether.

MAKE IT GLUTEN-FREE

Use gluten-free flour.

WHAT TO DO WITH LEFTOVERS

Spanakopita keeps for up to two weeks when refrigerated and covered or stored in an airtight container. My best advice is to try to enjoy as much as you can before refrigerating, as it never tastes as good afterwards. Once cooled, make sure to properly cover in plastic wrap and refrigerate.

Τυρόπιτα

Tiropita | Feta cheese pie

SERVES 6

FILLING
400 g (14 oz) Greek feta
   crumbled
4 large eggs, beaten
1 teaspoon freshly ground
   black pepper
500 g (18 oz) unsalted butter,
   melted

DOUGH
1.6 kg (3½ lb) special white
   flour, farina flour or
   00 plain flour, plus extra
   for dusting
3 tablespoons extra-virgin
   olive oil
750 ml (25½ fl oz/3 cups)
   lukewarm water
1 tablespoon sugar
¼ teaspoon vinegar
½ teaspoon salt

I love tiropita. This amazing swirling cheese pastry is such a stunning dish to share at any kitchen table. It can be enjoyed cold the next day and will keep easily for at least one week. While making the phyllo is time consuming, it is worth it, as the texture, taste and quality of the dish is so much deeper.

However, I know people can be time poor so if you do not have the time to make it, I would recommend buying a 375 g (13 oz) packet of thick Greek phyllo pastry. I recommend using the thick version of Antoniou Fillo Pastry .

I use special white flour, Greek farina flour and 00 Italian flour in all my handmade pastries. These specialty flours are more expensive than the standard plain flour you find in supermarkets but they are far superior. You can find them at any good Mediterranean deli. That being said, cost of living challenges are real and so you can use any flour and the dish will still be fine.

Preheat the oven to 180°C (360°F).

To make the dough, place the flour into a large bowl and make a well. Add 2 tablespoons of the olive oil, water, sugar, vinegar and salt.

Mix it together with your hands or with a wooden spoon.

Turn out the dough mixture onto a lightly floured surface and knead for about 5 minutes until the dough is soft and it bounces back when you press into it with your fingers.

Grease a large bowl with remaining olive oil, place dough in the bowl and cover with plastic wrap. Set aside in a warm place for an hour.

Combine crumbled Greek feta and beaten eggs in a shallow bowl and season well with freshly ground black pepper. Place butter in a second shallow bowl.

Turn out the dough onto a lightly floured surface and knead for 1–2 minutes.

Now roll the dough out into a cylinder shape. Divide it into 8 and roll each portion into a ball.

Add 1 dough round to the plate with the butter and turn to coat both sides in the butter. Repeat with remaining dough rounds, buttering each dough round on both sides and stacking each dough round on top of the other to create a stack similar to a stack of pancakes.

Using a rolling pin, roll out the stack into the widest and longest rectangular shape that you can.

Preheat the oven to 180°C (360°F) and grease a 30 cm (12 in) round tray with melted butter.

Spoon the feta, egg and pepper mixture along one long end of the pastry rectangle. Folding in the edges as you go, roll up the rectangle, starting from the long side, into a cigar-like shape. Transfer the pastry to the prepared tray and twirl into a spiral shape. Glaze with remaining melted butter and bake for about 45 minutes, or until golden brown.

IF YOU ARE USING STORE-BOUGHT PASTRY

Place 1 sheet of phyllo pastry on a flat work surface and brush with melted butter. Add a second sheet and brush with butter again. Spoon feta mixture along one long edge of the pastry sheet and roll up the pastry to form a long cigar-shape. Place in the centre of a greased 30 cm (12 in) round baking tray and twirl it into a little spiral. Now repeat again and each time wrap the next row of phyllo around the previous spiral on the baking tray, making it one large spiral until the baking tray is filled.

MAKE IT VEGAN

Replace the eggs with a vegan egg mix and replace feta and butter with vegan versions.

MAKE IT GLUTEN-FREE

Use a gluten-free phyllo pastry.

WHAT TO DO WITH LEFTOVERS

Use leftover tiropita mix by buttering and layering 4 layers of phyllo then placing leftover mixture in the middle, folding in the sides like a small parcel, and pan-frying in oil until golden.

Πεϊνιρλί

Peinirli – Greek pizzas four ways

SERVES 4

DOUGH
1 kg (2 lb 3 oz) 00 plain (all-purpose) flour, farina flour or special white flour, plus extra for dusting
2½ teaspoons yeast
2 teaspoons salt
1 teaspoon white or brown sugar
750 ml (25½ fl oz/3 cups) lukewarm water
extra-virgin olive oil, for glazing and greasing

ZUCCHINI AND HALLOUMI TOPPING
250 g (9 oz) halloumi, sliced
1 large zucchini (courgette), thinly sliced into circles
100 g (3½ oz) Greek feta, grated, to stuff the crust
25 g (1 oz) mint, finely chopped
1 lemon
1 pomegranate

SILVERBEET AND FETA TOPPING
400 g (14 oz) tinned crushed tomatoes
8 basil leaves
1 tablespoon dried Greek oregano
1 teaspoon sugar
1 tablespoon tomato paste
350 g (12½ oz) Greek feta
250 g (9 oz) silverbeet (Swiss chard), sautéed
2 red onions, sliced into rings

The Greek peinirli has its roots in the refugee story of Greece. It was a dish brought by refugees who fled the Ancient Greek city of Smyrna (now known as Izmir in modern-day Turkey after it was invaded and occupied) in 1922 after the Great Fire of Smyrna. Turkish forces set the Greek and Armenian quarters of the city alight, killing upwards of 100,000 people and displacing hundreds of thousands more as refugees.

It is a boat-shaped bread that can be filled with whatever your heart desires. I love to stuff the crust of my peinirli with crumbled Greek feta cheese. Kasseri would also work beautifully as a crust filling.

Preheat the oven to 200°C (390°F) and line a large baking tray with baking paper.

To make the dough, combine water, yeast and sugar in a bowl, cover with plastic wrap and set aside for 15 minutes to ferment. Using a wooden spoon or mixing with your hands, gradually add flour and salt and mix to combine.

Turn out dough onto a lightly floured surface and knead for 5 minutes until soft and springy – the dough should bounce back when you place your thumb into it.

Place in an oiled bowl, cover with plastic wrap (wrap also in a blanket or large towel if it is cold in your house) and set aside in a warm place for at least 2 hours to prove.

Turn out the dough onto a lightly floured surface and knead for a further 1–2 minutes. Divide into 4 equal portions.

Roll each dough ball out into the size of a little boat shape of about 30 cm (12 in) × 10 cm (4 in) wide.

Add your toppings through the centre of each dough, leaving the edges of the dough empty so we can fold them in later to create the boat-like pizzas.

KASSERI AND OLIVES TOPPING

400 g (14 oz) tinned crushed tomatoes

8 fresh basil leaves

1 tablespoon of dried Greek oregano

1 teaspoon of sugar

1 tablespoon of tomato paste

100 g (3½ oz) Greek feta, grated, to stuff the crust

250 g (9 oz) kasseri cheese, coarsely grated

200 g (7 oz) sliced black olives

1 teaspoon dried Greek oregano

CHERRY TOMATOES AND FETA TOPPING

250 g (9 oz) cherry tomatoes, halved

250 g (9 oz) Greek feta

1 tablespoon dried Greek oregano

Crumble Greek feta at the edges of the dough and fold them in to create a dough feta crust; in doing so you are now also encasing the toppings (the only one where I did not stuff the crust with feta was the cherry tomato and feta pizza, but you can stuff the crust on this one too if you like).

Now take each end of the dough, one at a time, and gently twirl as pictured. Brush the pastry with extra-virgin olive oil.

Place on a prepared tray and bake for 30–45 minutes until you get a golden crust and the cheese is melted and golden.

MAKE IT VEGAN

By using a vegan halloumi, feta, kasseri, mozzarella, colby, provolone or pecorino romano cheese.

MAKE IT GLUTEN-FREE

Use gluten-free flour.

WHAT TO DO WITH

LEFTOVERS

Few things beat cold pizza the next day. Am I right?

Τυροπιτάκια

Tiropitakia | Feta pies

SERVES 4

FILLING
2 eggs, beaten
200 g (7 oz) Greek feta, crumbled

DOUGH
400 g (14 oz) Greek-style yoghurt
250 ml (8½ fl oz/1 cup) canola oil
400 g (14 oz) self-raising (self-rising) flour, sifted
1 teaspoon salt
1 teaspoon sugar

GLAZE
1 egg yolk
1 teaspoon water

Our love of phyllo pastry, cheese pies and pies filled with wild greens began thousands of years ago. In the 5th century BC, poet Philoxenos wrote in his poems of milk, honey and cheese pies. The term phyllo in fact comes from the Greek word 'leaf'. Before that, we would bake thick porridge made from grains on hot stones to create flat breads. This evolved into sheets of phyllo pastry made from fat, olive oil and dough, and communities would fill the sheets with whatever wild greens they could grow or forage for.

Start by straining the yoghurt for 2 hours by either hanging yoghurt in a tea towel on a kitchen tap or lining a colander with a muslin cloth and leaving in your sink to strain.

To make the dough, combine oil, strained yoghurt, flour, salt and sugar in a bowl. Gently knead to form a dough, then set aside to rest for 10 minutes.

Preheat the oven to 180°C (360°F).

Combine egg and feta in a separate bowl.

Divide dough into about 20 portions and roll into circles about 4.5 cm (1¾ in) in diameter.

Spoon a little of the egg and feta mixture into the centre of each circle, then fold over and press the edges together firmly with the tines of a fork to seal.

Beat the egg yolk and water together and then use as a glaze to brush all over the tiropitakia. Bake for about 30 minutes, or until golden.

MAKE IT VEGAN

By using vegan feta, butter and Greek-style soy, plant-based or coconut yoghurt. Replace the eggs with a vegan egg mix or leave out.

MAKE IT GLUTEN-FREE

Use a gluten-free flour.

WHAT TO DO WITH LEFTOVERS

If you have any of the feta filling left over, chop up some spinach and silverbeet (Swiss chard), gently sauté and pour this over to make a terrific omelette.

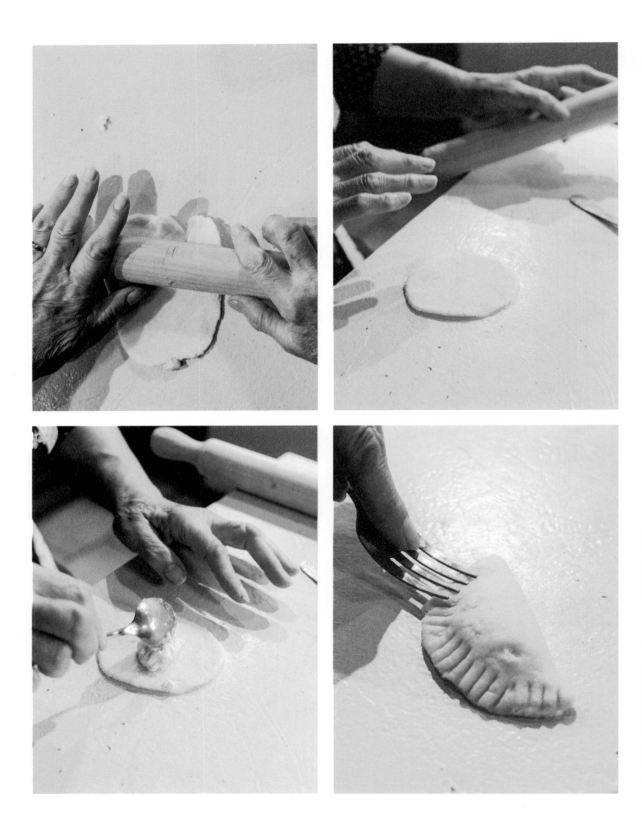

Ποντιακό πιροσκί

Pontian piroshki | Potato pies

SERVES 4

500 g (1 lb 2 oz) plain
(all purpose) flour
5 g dried yeast
1 teaspoon salt
80 ml (2½ fl oz/⅓ cup)
extra-virgin olive oil
1 egg, beaten
310 ml (10½ fl oz/1¼ cups)
lukewarm water
4 potatoes, quartered
1 red onion, chopped
15 g (½ oz/1 cup) flat-leaf
(Italian) parsley, finely
chopped
15 g (½ oz/¼ cup) mint,
finely chopped)
4 spring onions (scallions),
finely chopped
500 ml (17 fl oz/2 cups)
canola oil, for frying

MAKE IT VEGAN

By using a vegan egg mix instead
of eggs.

MAKE IT GLUTEN-FREE

By using a gluten-free flour.

WHAT TO DO WITH LEFTOVERS

The dough and potato mix can
easily be frozen in zip-lock plastic
bags, then defrosted overnight for
a further batch to be made in the
following weeks.

One of my deepest regrets is not ever asking my father, Leo,
about our Pontian history and culture and our food. I also lost
my Greek Pontian grandmother when I was in my early 20s so I
never got to learn any traditional Pontian recipes.

As I start my journey of reclaiming this part of me, I want to
share at least one traditional Pontian recipe in this cookbook.
This does not in any way do justice to a 3000-year-old culinary
history, however it is wonderful to share part of this story.

Combine flour, yeast and salt in a bowl. Add 2 tablespoons of
the olive oil and the egg and combine using a wooden spoon.

Gradually pour in the lukewarm water, slowly kneading until
dough forms a ball (you may not need to use all the water – if
the flour is flaky, add more water).

Put dough in a well-oiled bowl, cover with plastic wrap and set
aside to prove for 2 hours.

Once the dough has risen, cut dough into equal parts and roll
each part into a small ball. You should have 10 balls. Set them
aside on a tray and allow them to rise again for another hour.

To make the filling, bring a large saucepan of water to the boil.
Add potatoes and cook for 10–20 minutes, or until tender. Drain
and transfer to a large bowl and mash with a fork or potato
masher and set aside.

Heat remaining oil in a small frying pan and sauté onion for
2–3 minutes, or until tender. Add to the potatoes. Stir in the
parsley, mint and spring onions. Take one ball of dough and
flatten it with your hands, making a disc shape.

Using a spoon, scoop some of the potato filling into the centre
of the disc. Bring the edges of the disc together to seal the
potato dumpling.

Add enough canola oil to a large pot to come 6 cm (2½ in) up
the sides of the pot. Heat oil until hot.

Add piroshki to the pot, in small batches (do not overfill), and
cook for a few minutes, or until crisp and golden. Add more
canola oil if you need to as they absorb the oil. Once cooked,
transfer to a plate lined with a paper towel to drain excess oil.

Τηγανητός άνηθος και σπανακόπιτα της προγιαγιάς μου Γεωργίας

My great grandmother Georgia's fried dill and spinach pita

SERVES 4

1 onion, finely diced
60 g (2 oz/1 cup) dill,
    roughly chopped
500 g (1 lb 2 oz) spinach,
    roughly chopped
1 teaspoon cardamom seeds,
    toasted and finely ground
    in a mortar and pestle
1 teaspoon fennel seeds,
    toasted and finely ground
    in a mortar and pestle
salt and pepper, to taste
3 tablespoons extra-virgin
    olive oil
honey, for drizzling
sesame seeds, for sprinkling

DOUGH
500 g (1 lb 2 oz) plain
    (all-purpose) flour
pinch of sugar
pinch of salt
7 g (⅛ oz) sachet dried yeast
250 ml (8½ fl oz/1 cup)
    lukewarm water
1 tablespoon extra-virgin
    olive oil

You would ideally use Greek dill when making this recipe. It has a more intense flavour and can often be found when you're out walking, where you might see it growing in a park or on a pavement (or in the garden of a Greek neighbour). If you have no luck with that, regular dill will do.

Sauté onion, dill and spinach in a large frying pan over a medium heat for about 10 minutes, or until wilted.

Combine cardamom and fennel in a small bowl and season with salt and pepper.

To make the dough, combine flour, sugar, salt, yeast, warm water and oil in a bowl. Using your fingers, mix and knead gently to form a thick dough. Set aside for an hour to prove.

Cut the dough into balls of about 5 cm (2 in) diameter and then roll out one piece at a time to the size of a small circle.

Using your fingers, add a little of the spinach and dill mixture to the centre of each, taking care not to overfill. Fold the dough over to make an envelope.

Using a rolling pin, roll it lengthwise and crosswise until it is approximately 30 cm (12 in) × 10 cm (4 in) wide (be ready for it to squirt, so don't wear anything dear to you when making this!).

Heat oil in a frying pan over a high heat, add dough and fry for about 5 minutes on each side until golden. Drizzle with honey and sprinkle with sesame seeds to serve.

MAKE IT VEGAN
By using maple (or any vegan) syrup.

MAKE IT GLUTEN-FREE
Use a gluten-free flour.

WHAT TO DO WITH LEFTOVERS
Freeze the leftover dough in small rolls to use later for phyllo cheese pastries.

ACTION

I became a vegetarian at the age of 15 and have remained one. Why? I became passionate about human rights when I was a teenager, reading voraciously about the civil rights movement, the struggles to end apartheid and the women's rights movement for equality. It made me curious and I began questioning my relationship with animals, asking myself, 'Why do I eat them?' I felt that if I stood up for human rights, I should stand up for the rights of animals too. I decided just to stop eating meat or any animal with a face, and have never once looked back.

It is one of the best decisions I have ever made but was not without its dramas. I was the first in my family and among my relatives to become a vegetarian. It took a good two decades (I am not kidding) of me refusing offers of lamb, beef, chicken and fish at family gatherings for my relatives to accept that I was serious and it was not just a phase I was going through.

I wish I knew then what I know now, which is that the Ancient Greeks were some of the first proponents of vegetarianism, both as matters of health and justice. They saw animals as having a soul, just like us. Pythagoras (580 BC), following in the footsteps of the Egyptian and ancient Indian civilisations, taught that all animals should be treated as kindred, with a right to live in common with mankind. Pythagoras saw vegetarianism as essential to a peaceful human co-existence and healthy life. To slaughter animals was to brutalise the human soul, in his eyes.

Thousands of years have since passed and this truth has endured. Sadly it is one we have not heeded. We have a live animal export trade that is built on accepting the suffering of animals as they are sent across the globe to be killed for their meat. Millions of farmed animals are subjected to unimaginable cruelty and millions more are locked up in factory farms in appalling and inhumane conditions with no protections. This is further compounded by hunting and commercial killing of animals, as well as the impact of bushfires that are ravaging our native wildlife. As a society, our modern reliance on meat-based diets is having catastrophic impacts on our environment and the welfare of animals.

Educating the mind without educating the heart isn't education at all.

– ARISTOTLE

We are facing a climate emergency and reckoning with the catastrophic consequences of our dependency on a meat-based diet. While writing this book, I discovered to my shock that 80 per cent of the world's farmland is taken up by livestock as our most diverse and fragile natural wonders, including the Amazon jungle, are being deforested to create more land to farm animals.

I learnt that animal agriculture also uses 20–30 per cent of the world's fresh water while 60 per cent of our global fish populations are already fully fished, and declining, and another 30 per cent are overfished. This sounds completely unsustainable.

It came as an even bigger surprise to me to learn that cows and sheep produce about 37 per cent of the total methane generated by human activity. Methane is responsible for nearly half of the planet's human-induced global warming. That is just staggering to try to take in.

If we are to create a compassionate and kinder world, we need to be conscious of our impact on the planet and understand the profound link between farming animals and climate change, sustainable eating choices and protecting our one and only home.

The case for a plant-based diet is indeed irresistible. It's hard to take in the following figures but it makes me feel good to at least be reducing my footprint by being a vegetarian. We know it's large multinationals that are by far the biggest culprits, but it's affirming to know our individual choices can also make a difference.

A meat-based diet requires 17 times more land and 14 times more energy than a vegetarian diet. A vegetarian or vegan diet emits 2.5 times less carbon emissions than a meat-based diet. A vegan diet uses 75 per cent less land, one-fifth of the water and has much lower energy consumption than a meat-based diet. It has the lowest carbon footprint of any diet.

Going plant-based and vegan in your diet is like possessing a superpower to help the environment in such incredibly wide-ranging ways – most of which I had no idea about until I wrote this book, to be honest. It has inspired me to continue to move, as I have begun to do in recent years, to a predominately vegan diet.

A VEGAN DIET:

- reduces greenhouse gases and emissions
- reduces pressure on overfished oceans and energy consumption
- reduces the use of antibiotics, growth hormones and other chemicals that contribute to pharmaceutical pollution
- protects rainforests from deforestation, creates cleaner waterways
- preserves wild habitats and natural spaces, promotes cleaner soils
- protects endangered species and wildlife and helps reduce world hunger and biodiversity loss.

Since being a teenager, I have dreamed of a world where there was no such thing as hunger. In recent years, as climate change has ravaged the earth, and floods and droughts and the wars it has created have caused massive disruption to food security, I have felt like it was an impossible dream to realise. It feels impossible to realise it would take about 40 million tonnes of food to end the worst world hunger scenarios, and we are already using 760 million tonnes per annum of agricultural food just to feed animals for a meat-based diet. Imagine if we flipped our global priorities to ending world hunger rather than creating it.

We are all interconnected and we cannot forget this. What we consume and the choices we make have consequences for the planet every single day.

Ρόδι, τζατζίκι και πλατύφυλλο αγκινάρας

Pomegranate, tzatziki and artichoke flatbread

SERVES 4

FLATBREAD
1 kg (2 lb 3 oz) Greek-style
    yoghurt
1 teaspoon salt
2 teaspoon baking powder
1 kg (2 lb 3 oz) plain
    (all-purpose) flour, plus
    extra for dusting
250 ml (8½ fl oz/1 cup) canola
    oil, for frying
1 tablespoon Greek oregano

TOPPINGS
1 quantity Tzatziki (page 75)
handful of dill, chopped
handful of mint, chopped
300 g (10½ oz) artichoke
    hearts, sliced
200 g (7 oz) Greek feta,
    crumbled
1 pomegranate, halved
    and seeds reserved
extra-virgin olive oil,
    for drizzling

MAKE IT VEGAN
By using a Greek-style soy,
plant-based or coconut yoghurt
and vegan feta.

MAKE IT GLUTEN-FREE
Use gluten-free flour.

WHAT TO DO WITH LEFTOVERS
Repurpose the leftover toppings
into a delicious salad.

For me, the hero of this dish is the pomegranate seeds. Symbolising fertility in Ancient Greece, the pomegranate had ties to Aphrodite, goddess of love, and Dionysus, god of wine and pleasure. In Ancient Greece, smashing a pomegranate on New Year's Day served as a symbol of good fortune for the coming year. Today people know the pomegranate as one of the oldest superfoods. Make the tzatziki the night before so you can assemble these flatbreads more quickly.

TO MAKE THE FLATBREAD

Combine yoghurt, salt, baking powder and flour in a large bowl.

Turn out the mixture onto a lightly floured working surface and knead for 1 minute, or until smooth and elastic.

Place in a flour-dusted bowl, cover with a plate and set aside to rest for 30 minutes.

Cut the dough into small pieces (about 200–225 g/8 oz per dough ball) and roll out into the flatbreads of the size you would like.

Heat a few tablespoons of canola oil in a large saucepan or frying pan over a high heat. Cook dough, turning, until golden brown on both sides. Remove from the pan and sprinkle each with Greek oregano. Repeat with remaining dough, adding a few tablespoons of oil each time.

Spread the tzatziki all over each flatbread (about 3 tablespoons of tzatziki per flatbread). Top each with dill, mint, artichoke, crumbled feta and pomegranate seeds and finish with a drizzling of extra-virgin olive oil.

Λαγάνα

Lagana | Bread

SERVES 6

750 ml (25½ fl oz/3 cups)
   warm water
3 tablespoons dried yeast
1 tablespoon sugar
1 kg (2 lb 3 oz/7 cups)
   00 farina flour, plus extra
   for dusting
1 tablespoon salt
¼ teaspoon vinegar
2 tablespoons extra-virgin
   olive oil, plus extra for
   greasing and drizzling
sesame seeds, washed,
   drained and dried,
   for sprinkling (optional)

Our most famous bread in Greek cooking has its roots in Ancient Greece with first references to it dating back to the 5th century BC. It is incredibly popular leading up to Greek Easter, as part of Lent when Greeks fast for 40 days, and it is a bread which, while traditionally topped with sesame seeds as I have here, can also be covered with everything from olives to Greek oregano, thyme and rosemary.

An important step is to take it out of its baking tray and prop it up on its side against a wall, leaving it for up to an hour to fully set before eating. It is equally important to slice it into the shapes you want before baking it. We traditionally go with a diamond shape, cutting halfway down before baking.

Combine water, yeast and sugar in a bowl, cover with plastic wrap and leave for 15 minutes to ferment.

Combine the flour and salt in a large bowl, and make a well in the middle. Add yeast mixture to the centre of the well and, using your hands or a wooden spoon, gently fold in for 1 minute to combine. Add vinegar and oil and mix to combine.

Turn out the mixture onto a lightly floured surface and knead for 3–5 minutes to form a soft dough.

Grease the bowl with oil and return the dough to the bowl. Cover with plastic wrap and set aside in a warm place for 3 hours. If you have cold weather, wrap a blanket around the bowl to help heat it up to rise, making sure the blanket doesn't touch the dough mix.

Preheat the oven to 180°C (360°F).

Turn out dough onto a lightly floured surface and knead for a further 2 minutes.

Grease a large round baking tray with oil and place the dough on the tray. Flatten it with your hands so it covers the tray and is evenly spread.

Using your hands, oil the surface of the dough with extra-virgin olive oil (this will help give it its golden colour when baked). Using your fingers, place indents throughout the surface of the dough (as if you were making focaccia).

Sprinkle with sesame seeds, if you like, and bake for 1 hour until golden (about 10 minutes before the end of the cooking time, remove from the oven and, with your fingers, sprinkle cold water over the surface of the dough – this will help deepen the colour of the baked bread).

Once you have removed from the oven, gently take out from the pan and place the lagana on its side against a wall or a flat surface and leave for at least 30 minutes to rest before slicing to serve.

———

KON'S TIP: *Washing the sesame seeds in water, draining them and drying them on a tea towel before adding to the dough will stop the seeds from burning.*

MAKE IT VEGAN

It already is!

MAKE IT GLUTEN-FREE

By using a gluten-free flour.

WHAT TO DO WITH LEFTOVERS

Have it fresh or toasted with avocado or butter or olive oil, Greek oregano and feta for weeks to come.

Pasta, Rice & Legumes

Παστίτσιο

Pastitso | Baked pasta

SERVES 8

500 g (1 lb 2 oz) ziti pasta
1 tablespoon extra-virgin
    olive oil
100 g (3½ oz/1 cup) mizithra,
    finely grated
freshly grated nutmeg, to
    garnish
mizithra, finely grated,
    to garnish

TOMATO SAUCE
80 ml (2½ fl oz/⅓ cup)
    extra-virgin olive oil
1 onion, finely diced
1 teaspoon sugar
2 garlic cloves, finely chopped
4 carrots, grated
500 g (1 lb 2 oz) button
    mushrooms, roughly
    chopped
1 teaspoon sweet paprika
½ teaspoon ground cinnamon
½ teaspoon ground nutmeg
4 cloves
100 ml (3½ fl oz) red wine
800 g (1 lb 12 oz) tinned
    diced tomatoes
1 tablespoon tomato paste
500 ml (17 fl oz/2 cups) water
salt and pepper, to taste

This is one of my all-time favourite Greek dishes; it fills the heart and soul. Think of a lasagne – but even better, with its layered ziti pasta, béchamel, mizithra and rich tomato sauce. Pastitso has its origins in Italian cooking, from the pasticcio. This dish was created by the Greek chef Nikolaos Tselementes, who was the creator of not just pastitso but also the moussaka, which makes him a Greek cooking god! He published one of the first modern Greek cookbooks, back in the 1930s, and was credited with bringing French cooking techniques and recipes into Greek cooking as you can see with the béchamel sauce in this dish.

TO MAKE THE TOMATO SAUCE

To make the tomato sauce, heat the olive oil in a large frying pan over a low heat. Sauté onion and sugar until onion is softened. Add garlic, carrot, mushroom, paprika, cinnamon, nutmeg and cloves and stir until combined. Add red wine and cook, stirring, until the wine has evaporated. Add tinned tomatoes, tomato paste and water, then season with salt and pepper and cook for 45 minutes.

TO MAKE THE BÉCHAMEL SAUCE

To make the béchamel sauce, melt the butter in a medium-sized pot, then gradually add the flour and stir constantly until it thickens and forms a paste. Gradually add the milk, stirring constantly over a medium heat until it thickens into a thick sauce. Now stir through the grated kasseri and mizithra, crack eggs in and stir through. Season with pepper and set aside.

Preheat the oven to 180°C (360°F).

Bring a large pot of water to boil and cook ziti pasta until al dente, then drain and set aside, stirring in 1 tablespoon of extra-virgin olive oil to prevent it from sticking.

BÉCHAMEL SAUCE

250 g (9 oz) unsalted butter

90 g (3 oz) plain (all-purpose) flour

1.5 litres (51 fl oz/6 cups) milk

250 g (9 oz) unsalted butter

150g (5½ oz/1 cup) kasseri cheese, grated

35g (1½ oz/⅓ cup) mizithra, finely grated

2 eggs

pepper, to taste

TO ASSEMBLE

Spoon a little of the tomato sauce into the base of a deep 30 cm (12 in) baking tray or roasting tin, covering it all to avoid the pastitso sticking during baking.

Now top the cooked pasta with 5 tablespoons of grated mizithra, followed by one-third of the béchamel sauce. Toss through with a spoon (or your hands, if it's not too hot for you). This will add flavour to each layer.

Next, take some of the pasta and layer it until you have covered the baking tray. Cover with tomato sauce, then dollop about 6 teaspoons of the béchamel sauce across the layer. Sprinkle all over with 1 tablespoon of mizithra. Repeat until you have used all of the pasta, tomato sauce and béchamel sauce.

Top with grated nutmeg and mizithra and bake for 70–90 minutes until deep golden brown. A tip is to put a knife in and pull it out and if the mixture is really sticking to the knife it means it needs to be cooked a little longer. Another tip is to cook it fully covered with aluminium foil for the first 45 minutes and then remove the foil to allow it to cook inside before getting too much colour.

MAKE IT VEGAN

Substitute the butter for extra-virgin olive oil or a vegan butter. Leave out egg and use soy milk and vegan parmesan instead.

MAKE IT GLUTEN-FREE

Use a gluten-free flour and pasta.

WHAT TO DO WITH LEFTOVERS

If you have leftover ziti pasta, slice it into the size you want and then fry up some garlic and onion in olive oil. Add any leftover veggies you have in the fridge (such as capsicum/bell peppers, broccoli, mushrooms or zucchini/courgette) with a little red wine. Toss pasta through until warm and finish with some grated mizithra.

Χωριάτικη σαλάτα ζυμαρικών

Greek pasta salad

SERVES 6

500 g (1 lb 2 oz) fusilli pasta
60 ml (2 fl oz/¼ cup)
    extra-virgin olive oil,
    finely chopped
30 g (1 oz/1 cup) flat-leaf
    (Italian) parsley, finely
    chopped
20 g (1 oz/1 cup) mint
2 red capsicums (bell peppers),
    deseeded and sliced
2 red onions, cut into wedges
100 g (3½ oz) pitted olives
80 ml (2½ fl oz/⅓ cup) white
    vinegar
juice of 1 lemon
200 g (7 oz) cherry or baby
    roma tomatoes (red or
    multicoloured), halved
150 g (5½ oz) semi-dried
    tomatoes
1 teaspoon dried Greek
    oregano
2 Lebanese cucumbers,
    chopped
salt and pepper, to taste
100 g (3½ oz) Greek feta

I love this salad – it is spring and summer in a bowl. The contrast of these bright vegetables with the pasta tossed with fresh herbs and generous amounts of olive oil go perfectly together. You can also replace fusilli pasta with penne, macaroni or hilopites pasta.

Bring a large saucepan of salted water to the boil. Cook pasta until al dente, drain and set aside to cool.

Combine oil, herbs, capsicum, onion, olives, vinegar, lemon juice, tomatoes, Greek oregano and cucumber in a large bowl and season with salt and pepper. Add pasta and toss through to combine. Season well and sprinkle with feta to serve.

MAKE IT VEGAN

It already is! If using feta, choose a vegan feta.

MAKE IT GLUTEN-FREE

By using a gluten-free pasta.

WHAT TO DO WITH LEFTOVERS

All pasta salads can become delicious Greek pasta bakes. First, drain salad, toss with grated hard cheese, finish with a sprinkle of extra cheese on top and bake at 180°C (360°F) until golden.

Χυλοπίτες

Hilopites | Handmade egg pasta

SERVES 4

500 g (1 lb 2 oz) hilopites

4 tablespoons extra-virgin olive oil

4 garlic cloves, finely diced

100 g (3½ oz) butter

4 teaspoons finely chopped flat-leaf (Italian) parsley

1 teaspoon chicken-flavoured vegan stock powder

1 teaspoon sweet paprika

1 teaspoon dried Greek oregano

100 g (3½ oz/1 cup) mizithra, finely grated

Hilopites are the small, square-shaped egg noodles often found in Greek dishes. My mum tells me that in her hometown there would be dedicated days for making hilopites, where local women would each take turns in helping each other make enough hilopites to last through the winter. They would be freshly made each summer and left out in a sunny part of the house to dry for a week. My yiayia Olga would then fill pillowcases with them, to have them ready for the long winter months.

Bring a large pot of salted water to the boil and cook hilopites until al dente (about 15 minutes), drain and set aside.

In the same pot over a low heat, heat olive oil and cook garlic for 1 minute. Add butter and cook until melted. Add half the parsley, the stock powder, sweet paprika and Greek oregano and cook, stirring, for 2 minutes.

Stir in half the mizithra and fry for another 2 minutes. Add cooked hilopites and cook, stirring continuously, for a further 2 minutes. Garnish with remaining parsley, oregano and mizithra to serve.

TO HAND MAKE THE HILOPITES

In a bowl, sift 450 g (1 lb/3 cups) 00 plain (all-purpose) flour with 1 teaspoon of salt.

Create a well in the flour and add 5 eggs.

Gently mix in 500 ml (17 fl oz/2 cups) full-cream (whole) milk, kneading mixture into a thick dough. Cut off a handful and roll out as thin as you can, as though making a square pizza. Using your hand as a ruler, and using a sharp knife, slice long, thin slices of pasta. Cook in salted boiling water until al dente. Cool, then cut them into squares of any size you like.

MAKE IT VEGAN

Replace the eggs with a vegan egg mix and use vegan parmesan instead of mizithra.

MAKE IT GLUTEN-FREE

By using a gluten-free flour.

WHAT TO DO WITH LEFTOVERS

Fry up some capsicum (bell pepper), olives, capers, parsley and mint in olive oil and fry the leftover hilopites in them for a couple of minutes.

Χωριάτικη σαλάτα με κριθαράκι

Orzo salad

SERVES 6

500 g (1 lb 2 oz) orzo pasta
250 g (9 oz) cherry tomatoes, halved
2 cucumbers, diced
100 g (3½ oz) Kalamata olives, chopped (optional)
20 g (¾ oz/1 cup) mint, chopped
30 g (1 oz/1 cup) flat-leaf (Italian) parsley, chopped
100 g (3½ oz) Greek feta, crumbled (optional)
2 tablespoons white vinegar
4 tablespoons extra-virgin olive oil
2 red capsicums (bell peppers), thinly sliced
2 yellow capsicums (bell peppers), thinly sliced
2 red onions, cut into thin wedges
juice of 1 lemon
1 teaspoon dried Greek oregano
4 spring onions (scallions), thinly sliced
salt and pepper, to taste

MAKE IT VEGAN
Use vegan feta.

MAKE IT GLUTEN-FREE
Use gluten-free orzo pasta.

WHAT TO DO WITH LEFTOVERS
Place the leftover pasta in a baking dish and mix in some beaten eggs and finish with grated kaseri or kefalograviera, crumbled feta or any grated hard cheese and then top with a béchamel sauce and bake until golden brown.

You will find orzo pasta most commonly used in the very popular dish youvetsi, where it's cooked with beef, spices and a rich tomato sauce, and kritharaki, where orzo is cooked in a rich tomato sauce. Here I have made it as a salad, which is another popular way to cook this pasta in Greek cuisine.

Bring a large saucepan of salted water to the boil and cook orzo pasta for about 10 minutes, or until al dente. Drain, and set aside to cool, then transfer to a large bowl. Add all remaining ingredients, season to taste and gently toss to combine.

Πρασόριζο

Prasorizo | Leeks and rice

SERVES 4

80 ml (2½ fl oz/⅓ cup)
   extra-virgin olive oil
1 onion, diced
1 teaspoon sugar
3 spring onions (scallions),
   diced
3 leeks, sliced
100 g (3½ oz/½ cup)
   long grain rice
60 g (2 oz/1 cup), chopped
   dill, plus extra to serve
250 ml (8½ fl oz/1 cup) water
salt and pepper, to taste
juice of 1 lemon
Greek feta, crumbled,
   to serve

Prasorizo is a delicious, rustic vegan Greek rice dish made with leeks (praso) and rice (rizo). This humble dish is a delicious superfood as it is high in magnesium and vitamins A, C and K. It is the caramelisation of the leeks in this dish that give it its rich, sweet and creamy flavour. This is one of the most popular dishes in Greece in the lead up to Easter during our 40 days of fasting without dairy or meat. You can eat it both warm and at room temperature.

Heat olive oil in a large frying pan over a low heat. Add onion, sugar and spring onion and cook for 2–3 minutes, stirring occasionally.

Add the leek and sauté for a further 5 minutes, or until softened, taking care not to burn. Add rice and dill and continue cooking for another 2 minutes.

Add water, season with salt and pepper, bring to boil and then reduce to a simmer and cook for 20–25 minutes, stirring, or until all the liquid is absorbed. Remove from heat and stir through lemon juice, extra dill and feta to serve.

MAKE IT VEGAN
   Use a vegan feta.

MAKE IT GLUTEN-FREE
   It already is!

WHAT TO DO WITH LEFTOVERS
   Crack in some eggs, flour and
   breadcrumbs and make into little
   rice patties and fry.

Κριθαράκι

Kritharaki | Orzo and tomato

SERVES 4

500 g (1 lb 2 oz) orzo pasta
80 ml (2½ fl oz/⅓ cup)
   extra-virgin olive oil
1 onion, diced
1 teaspoon sugar
3 garlic cloves, crushed
200 g (7 oz) tinned diced
   tomatoes
1 teaspoon tomato paste
400 ml (13½ fl oz) water
1 teaspoon sweet paprika
3 cloves
½ teaspoon freshly grated
   nutmeg
½ teaspoon vegetable stock
   powder
salt and pepper, to taste
50 g (1¾ oz) mizithra, grated

Greek orzo is similar to Italian orzo pasta, however it is slightly larger, takes longer to cook and is made from a different type of wheat. We call it kritharaki, which means 'little barley'. In Greek culture, we love to use this pasta for a wide variety of dishes, from cooking it vegan-style with tomato sauce to serving it with shellfish, beef or chicken, or as a salad with roasted vegetables, feta or halloumi.

Bring a large saucepan of water to the boil. Cook pasta until al dente. Drain and set aside.

Heat oil in a large frying pan over a low heat. Sauté onion and sugar until soft. Add garlic and cook for another minute, then add tinned tomatoes, tomato paste, water, paprika, cloves, nutmeg, vegetable stock and salt and pepper to taste. Cook on low heat for 20 minutes, or until the sauce thickens. Stir in the cooked pasta and finish with grated mizithra. Set aside to stand for at least 10 minutes so the pasta can absorb the sauce.

MAKE IT VEGAN

Use vegan hard cheese.

MAKE IT GLUTEN-FREE

Use gluten-free orzo pasta.

WHAT TO DO WITH LEFTOVERS

You can easily repurpose the leftovers into rice patties. Add flour, eggs, breadcrumbs and dust in a plate of flour and fry.

Σπανακόριζο

Spanakorizo | Spinach and dill rice

SERVES 4

120 ml (2½ fl oz) extra-virgin
  olive oil, plus extra
  (optional) for drizzling
1 brown onion, finely diced
1 teaspoon sugar
2 leeks, finely diced
1½ bunches (400 g/14 oz)
  English spinach, roughly
  chopped
100 g (3½ oz/¾ cup)
  medium-grain rice
2–3 spring onions (scallions),
  finely sliced
250 ml (8½ fl oz/1 cup) water
15 g (1 oz/½ cup) flat-leaf
  (Italian) parsley, chopped
30 g (1 oz/½ cup) dill,
  chopped
salt and pepper, to taste
juice of 1½ lemons
50–100 g (1 3/4 oz–3 1/2
  oz) Greek feta (optional),
  to garnish

Spanakoprizo is a dish I make dozens of times each year. It's quick, simple, cheap and so healthy. This rice pilaf dish is made in every Greek home and it is one of our most loved meals. Here I have made it sketo (that means 'white', i.e. without a tomato-based sauce), however the tomato version is just as good (just add 200 g/2½ fl oz of crushed tinned tomatoes and 1 tablespoon of tomato paste). You can also add more spinach if you want an even greener pilaf. I also like to add silverbeet (Swiss chard), freshly squeezed lemon juice and plenty of Greek feta.

Heat 4 tablespoons of the oil in a large pot over a medium heat. Add onion and sugar and cook for 2 minutes. Add leek and cook for a further 3 minutes, or until softened. Add spinach and remaining olive oil. Cover pot, reduce heat to low and cook for a further 3–4 minutes, or until wilted. Using a wooden spoon, stir in rice and cook for a further 3 minutes. Add spring onion and cook for 1 minute. Add the water, bring to the boil, then reduce to a simmer, cover with lid and cook for 10 minutes. Add herbs, season to taste and cook for a further minute.

Remove from heat and stir in lemon juice. Set aside to stand for 10 minutes before serving (this allows the rice to fluff up and the lemon to infuse the dish). If you like, sprinkle with crumbled feta and drizzle with oil to serve.

MAKE IT VEGAN

It already is!

MAKE IT GLUTEN-FREE

It already is!

WHAT TO DO WITH LEFTOVERS

Have them for breakfast the next morning on toasted bread with grated kasseri, kefalograviera or feta.

Τηγανητό ρύζι με δυόσμο, άνηθο, μαϊντανό, λεμόνι και κουκιά

Fried rice with herbs, lemon and broad beans

SERVES 4

500 g (1 lb 2 oz) fresh broad beans, podded and peeled
80 ml (2½ fl oz/⅓ cup) extra-virgin olive oil, plus extra for drizzling
2 onions, grated
200 g (7 oz/1 cup) jasmine rice
10 g (¼ oz/½ cup) mint, finely chopped
15 g (½ oz/½ cup) flat-leaf (Italian) parsley, finely chopped
30 g (1 oz/½ cup) dill, finely chopped
170 ml (5½ fl oz) water
salt and pepper, to taste
juice of 1 lemon

Traditionally, it was bulgur and trahana rather than rice that Greeks would turn to for their soups and stews, and for things such as stuffing vegetables and making pilaf. Rice is mainly grown in the region near where my father, Leo, is from, the magnificent city of Thessaloniki. In this dish, I combine fried rice with broad beans, lemon and fresh herbs, which all go perfectly together. However, you could just as easily mix it with sautéed spinach and silverbeet (Swiss chard) or with peas and halloumi or roasted eggplant (aubergine) and zucchini (courgette).

Bring a large saucepan of water to the boil, add beans and cook for 5 minutes. Drain and set aside.

Heat oil in a large frying pan over a low heat. Sauté onion for about 2 minutes, or until softened. Add rice and cook for 3 minutes. Stir in herbs and cook for 1 minute. Add the water and cook for 5–10 minutes, or until liquid is absorbed.

Now place into a bowl and toss together with the broad beans. Season with salt and pepper and lemon juice and drizzle with olive oil to serve.

MAKE IT VEGAN

It already is!

MAKE IT GLUTEN-FREE

It already is!

WHAT TO DO WITH LEFTOVERS

You can easily repurpose this dish by serving the leftover rice with any of the delicious vegetable stews in this book or make it into rice keftedes by mixing with eggs, breadcrumbs and flour and frying.

Ρεβιθάδα

Chickpea stew

SERVES 4

500 g (1 lb 2 oz) dried
    chickpeas, soaked
    overnight, drained
    and rinsed
80 ml (2½ fl oz/⅓ cup)
    extra-virgin olive oil, plus
    extra (optional) for drizzling
1 onion, diced
2 spring onions (scallions),
    sliced
1 carrot, diced
250 g (2½ fl oz) silverbeet
    (Swiss chard), chopped
250 g (2½ fl oz) English
    spinach, chopped
handful of fresh dill
juice of 1 lemon
salt and pepper, to taste

This stew is not only cheap, easy and quick to make but it's packed with goodness, with the chickpeas and greens bringing tons of vitamins and health benefits. This is one of my go-to dishes when I need food that nurtures me and gives me energy all at once.

Bring a large pan of water to the boil, add chickpeas and cook for 30 minutes. Drain, rinse and set aside.

Heat olive oil in a large frying pan over a medium heat. Add onion, spring onion and carrot and cook for 5 minutes. Add chickpeas and pour in enough water to cover them, then cook for 20 minutes. Add silverbeet, spinach and dill and cook for a further 10 minutes. Add lemon juice, season to taste and drizzle with extra-virgin olive oil to serve.

MAKE IT VEGAN

It already is!

MAKE IT GLUTEN-FREE

It already is!

WHAT TO DO WITH LEFTOVERS

You can drain the stew (use the juices as a cooking base sauce for a pasta or bean stew) and then, using a fork, smash all the chickpeas, place leftovers in a bowl, add breadcrumbs, eggs and a little flour and make into a keftedes mix; refrigerate for a few hours and then dust in plain flour and fry.

Στιφάδο με μαυρομάτικα φασόλια και μπιζέλια

Black-eyed pea stew

SERVES 6

600 g (1 lb 5 oz/3 cups) dried black-eyed peas, soaked overnight

80 ml (2½ fl oz/⅓ cup) extra-virgin olive oil

1 onion, finely diced

1 teaspoon sugar

250 g (9 oz) silverbeet (Swiss chard), roughly chopped

250 g (9 oz) spinach, roughly chopped

3 spring onions (scallions), finely diced

15 g (½ oz/¼ cup) dill, finely chopped

15 g (½ oz/¼ cup) mint, finely chopped

7 g (½ oz/¼ cup) flat-leaf (Italian) parsley, finely chopped

2 tablespoons tomato paste

250 ml (8½ fl oz/1 cup) tinned crushed tomatoes

80 ml (2½ fl oz/⅓ cup) water

The queen of legumes is the black-eyed pea, for its versatility, taste and beauty. Black-eyed peas can be enjoyed in so many ways. You can boil them and simply toss with white vinegar, olive oil, diced onions and fresh herbs or mash them and mix with eggs, breadcrumbs and feta to make a fantastic black-eyed pea pattie. Or toss into a salad with roasted cherry tomatoes, feta, spring onions, red onions and mint. Here I make it as a delicious stew with greens and lots of fresh herbs.

Fill a large pot with water and bring to the boil. Add peas and cook for about 1 hour, or until tender but still firm. Drain and rinse gently under cold water and set aside.

Heat oil in a medium-sized pot over a low heat and sauté the onion and sugar for 2–3 minutes, or until caramelised. Add silverbeet and spinach and cook for 15 minutes until wilted. Add spring onion and herbs and cook for another couple of minutes.

Add tomato paste, tinned tomatoes, water and cook, gently stirring, for 10 minutes. Add beans and cook on low heat for about another 10 minutes until you get a lovely thick sauce and stew. Season to taste with salt and pepper about 5 minutes before the end of the cooking time.

MAKE IT VEGAN

It already is!

MAKE IT GLUTEN-FREE

It already is!

WHAT TO DO WITH LEFTOVERS

Drain the juices and put the leftovers in a large bowl. Using a hand mixer, blitz to create a delicious, thick black-eyed pea and spinach dip.

Σαλάτα με μαυρομάτικα φασόλια

Black-eyed pea salad

SERVES 6

500 g (1 lb 2 oz) black-eyed
    peas, soaked overnight
    and cooked until firm
    but tender, cooled
2 red onions, 1 diced and
    1 sliced into rings
3 spring onions (scallions),
    diced
1 yellow capsicum (bell
    pepper), diced
1 red capsicum (bell pepper),
    diced
4 tablespoons flat-leaf (Italian)
    parsley chopped
80 ml (2½ fl oz/⅓ cup)
    extra-virgin olive oil
4 teaspoons red-wine vinegar
100 g (3½ oz) green olives,
    pitted
60 g (2 oz) capers, drained
salt and pepper, to taste

You will see beans featured prominently throughout my cookbook. This is because legumes are such an important part of the Greek diet, in soups such as fakes, revithia and fasolatha and in dips, fritters and salads. I know people can be time-poor and not have the time to soak beans overnight or boil them before using. In this case, you can use tinned versions – just make sure to give them a really thorough wash in a colander, as they may contain preservatives and excess salt. If using tinned beans, you may find you need to add less salt.

Fill a large pot with water and bring to boil. Add the peas and cook for about 1 hour, or until tender but still firm. Drain, wash gently under cold water and set aside to cool.

Making this salad is as simple as combining all of the ingredients and tossing together.

MAKE IT VEGAN
    It already is!

MAKE IT GLUTEN-FREE
    It already is!

WHAT TO DO WITH LEFTOVERS
    Drain juices and blend the leftovers
    to create a flavoursome black-eyed
    pea dip.

Sweets & Drinks

Τηγανίτες

Tiganites | Greek pancakes

SERVES 4

750 ml (25½ fl oz/3 cups) lukewarm water

2½ teaspoons yeast

1 teaspoon white or brown sugar

1 kg (2 lb 3 oz) 00 flour, plus extra for dusting

2 teaspoons salt

2 tablespoons extra-virgin olive oil, plus extra for greasing

250 g (9 oz) Greek feta, crumbled

2 eggs, beaten

125 ml (4 fl oz/½ cup) canola oil

200 g (7 oz) honey (or as much as you like)

MAKE IT VEGAN

By using a vegan Greek feta and date or maple syrup instead of honey.

MAKE IT GLUTEN-FREE

By just using a gluten-free flour.

WHAT TO DO WITH LEFTOVERS

With leftover dough, cut into single-serve balls and place in zip-lock bags; freeze if not using anytime soon, otherwise it will keep in the fridge for a week.

This dish originates from the ancient griddle-cake dish called teganitai – it's been enjoyed by Greeks for thousands of years and is thought to be the world's first recorded version of pancakes!

It is incredibly versatile – you can top it with crushed walnuts or pistachio nuts, or even stuff it with chocolate. I love this version the most, as you have a wonderful contrast between the saltiness of the feta and the sweetness of the honey.

Combine water, yeast and sugar in a large bowl and set aside for 15 minutes. Gradually sift in the flour and the salt and add the oil. Using your hands, mix to combine, then roll the dough into a ball. Transfer to a lightly floured bench and knead for 5–7 minutes until you get a lovely soft dough that bounces back when you put your thumb into it (don't overdo it, you do not want it to get dry).

Place the dough in a well-oiled bowl, cover with plastic wrap and set aside in a warm place to prove for at least 2 hours.

Once the dough has doubled in size, return your dough to a lightly floured surface and gently knead. Divide into 140–150 g balls.

Roll each dough ball out into small rounds like pizzas. (Keep the dough pieces you are not using covered with a wet tea towel so they do not dry out.)

Scatter each with a little feta and beaten egg. Take the edges of your dough and bring it into the centre like you are folding and wrapping a present. Now roll into a circle again by very gently rolling out with your rolling pin.

You can even put a small bowl over your dough (be careful not to cut into the dough) to help you get the circle shape you want.

Prick each dough half a dozen times with your fork to make it easier to fry and cook the feta and egg inside.

Heat 60 ml (2 fl oz/¼ cup) of the canola oil in a large frying pan until hot. Add dough parcels, in batches, adding 60 ml (2 fl oz/¼ cup) of the canola oil each time, and cook for 2–3 minutes on both sides until golden. Note that the longer you are frying, the hotter the pan will get, so they may increasingly take less time, and you will need to keep a close eye on them to ensure they don't burn. Drizzle with honey to serve.

Γαλακτομπούρεκο

Galaktoboureko | Custard pie

SERVES 10 TO 12

250 g (9 oz) butter, melted
375 g (12½ oz) Greek
    phyllo pastry (about
    18–22 sheets)
ground cinnamon, for
    sprinkling

CUSTARD FILLING
1.5 litres (51 fl oz/6 cups) milk
220 g (8½ fl oz/1 cup) sugar
125 g (4½ oz/1 cup) fine
    semolina
1 teaspoon vanilla extract
zest of ½ lemon
3 eggs, beaten
40 g (1½ oz) unsalted butter

SYRUP
440 g (15½ oz/2 cups) white
    (granulated) sugar
250 ml (8½ fl oz/1 cup) water
2 cloves
½ lemon

I have childhood memories of my mum, Sia, making galaktoboureko as a special treat for us, and till this day it remains a special treat. This semolina custard baked in phyllo with a sugary sweet syrup is dessert heaven. Remember when making this dish that either the phyllo or the syrup must be cold and the other hot when you pour the syrup all over the pastry. When I am pouring the syrup, I love to bend down and listen to the dish as the hot phyllo and cold syrup meet together and you can hear it crackle. The longer you leave the syrup to sit in the phyllo before eating, the sweeter and better it is to eat.

To make the custard filling, gently heat milk in a medium pot or saucepan over a low heat. Add sugar after milk has heated, and stir until dissolved. Gradually pour in the semolina, stirring with a wooden spoon, until the mixture starts to simmer and thicken. Add vanilla and lemon zest and continue to cook, continuously stirring, until the mixture is thick like a béchamel sauce (if it does not thicken, add more semolina). Remove from heat.

Add eggs, stirring, then add butter and stir until thick, soft and smooth. If the mixture is a bit too thick, you can add a little more milk and keep stirring until it becomes nice and soft.

Brush a deep baking tray (I used one that was about 33 cm/13 in × 24 cm/9½ in and 7 cm/2¾ in high) with the melted butter. Arrange 8 phyllo sheets over the base of the baking tray. As you lay each phyllo sheet, drop the melted butter all over each sheet in dollops rather than brushing it (if you brush the butter on the phyllo, it will stick and won't make it fluffy).

Once you have laid half the sheets on the tray, spread with all the custard filling. Repeat the process with 8 more phyllo sheets, dotting with melted butter as you go, keeping 1 sheet aside to finish.

Now you will have the bottom and top phyllo sheets hanging over the edges of your baking tray, as they will be wider than it. Take any sheets that hang over and cut them off with a small sharp knife and then fold any final rough edges into the dish and use your brush to butter them all over to keep them in place.

Now to make your dish look beautiful and hide these rough leftover parts, you will add one final phyllo sheet on top. Fold underneath any excess phyllo or cut using a small sharp knife. If there is still any part overhanging the tray, cut so you have a nice even top that covers the whole dish. Now butter over all of this final phyllo sheet using your brush.

An important final step is to cut the galaktoboureko into the shape and size you want, as you can't do this once baked.

Preheat the oven to 180°C (360°F). Bake for 40–50 minutes until golden.

Meanwhile, prepare your syrup, combine all ingredients in a small saucepan over a medium heat, bring to a simmer and cook for 5 minutes, or until sugar is dissolved. Remove the lemon from the syrup.

Remember, for best results, your syrup must be cold and your pastry hot.

My mum's tip is to make the syrup and let it cool while the pastry is cooking, then it's ready to pour over once it is fresh out of the oven. Allow the pastry to sit for 2 minutes, then pour the cold syrup all over slowly and, using kitchen gloves, gently shake the tray side to side to help it absorb. Leave for a little to let the syrup soak in, then sprinkle with ground cinnamon to serve.

MAKE IT VEGAN

Replace the eggs with a vegan egg mix or omit, and use soy milk or almond milk and vegan butter.

MAKE IT GLUTEN-FREE

Use gluten-free phyllo pastry.

WHAT TO DO WITH LEFTOVERS

Seal the leftovers in plastic containers and refrigerate; the leftovers will still be fine to enjoy for the week to come.

Μελομακάρονα

Melomakarona | Honey cookies

SERVES 10 TO 12

SYRUP
500 ml (17 fl oz/2 cups) water
440 g (15½ oz/2 cups) white (granulated) sugar
¼ lemon with skin on
2 cloves
1 cinnamon stick
750 g (1 lb 11 oz/2 cups) honey

COOKIES
250 ml (8½ fl oz/1 cup) canola oil
220 g (8 oz/1 cup) white sugar
1 tablespoon orange zest
250 ml (8½ fl oz fl oz/1 cup) freshly squeezed orange juice
2 tablespoons brandy or cognac
½ teaspoon ground cinnamon
200 g (7 oz/2 cups) walnut halves, finely chopped
½ teaspoon bicarbonate of soda (baking soda)
1 teaspoon baking powder
1 kg (2 lb 3 oz) self-raising (self-rising) flour
230 g (8 oz/2 cups) finely ground walnuts
1 tablespoon ground cinnamon
½ teaspoon clove powder

Melomakaronas are a traditional Greek Christmas cookie infused with a delicate balance of orange, nutmeg, cinnamon, clove and walnuts. The word Melomakarona is derived from the Greek word for honey, 'meli'. These honey biscuits have their origins in the time of the Byzantine Empire.

With sweets, to double the amount of biscuits just double all the ingredients below. This is a safe rule of thumb for all Greek sweets in this book.

TO MAKE THE COOKIES

In a stand mixer set to high or speed 10, beat the oil and sugar for about 5 minutes until it becomes thicker with a bit of white colour.

Reduce the mixer to a low speed (or speed 2), add orange zest, orange juice, brandy and cinnamon and mix for 5 minutes. Add walnuts and mix for another minute then turn the mixer off and remove the bowl from the mixer.

Add the bicarbonate of soda to the bowl and mix in with a wooden spoon. Sift in the baking powder with 150 g (5½ oz/1 cup) of the flour. Gradually sift in 525 g (1 lb 3 oz/3½ cups) of the flour, mixing it with a wooden spoon to form a dough.

Turn out the dough onto a flat surface and gradually sift in the remaining flour, kneading as you go for a further 5 minutes to form a soft dough. Be careful to not overwork the dough. We just want it to absorb the flour, you will know you are overworking it if your dough gets really oily.

You can test if ready by pressing in a finger or thumb into the dough and seeing if it bounces right back.

Preheat the oven to 180°C (360°F) and line a baking tray with baking paper.

Cut the dough into small walnut-sized pieces.

Make them into small ovals as pictured here, about 4 cm (1½ in) long × 1.5 cm (½ in) wide.

Place on the prepared tray, making sure to have spacing between them each as they will spread during cooking. Using a fork, press along the biscuit to create a design for walnut and honey to be absorbed later or use a knife to cut three indents as pictured here on each biscuit. These indents are important as they are key to the biscuits being able to fully absorb the syrup.

Bake for about 45 minutes until golden then set aside to cool.

Crush the walnuts in a mortar and pestle until fine and then add the clove and cinnamon powder and stir through. Set aside.

TO MAKE THE SYRUP

Combine ingredients in a saucepan over a low heat and bring to the boil. Cook for 5 minutes, scooping off any white residue from the honey. Remove from heat and keep warm (you need the syrup to be hot when you dip the biscuits).

Drop each biscuit into the syrup, around 5 at a time, and use a spatula to turn them to ensure each side absorbs honey. Allow them to absorb the honey for about 5–6 seconds on each side then remove and transfer to a serving plate (don't leave them in the honey too long or they will break).

Sprinkle with walnut and cinnamon mixture to serve.

MAKE IT VEGAN

By using maple, date or dandelion syrup, vegan honey or agave nectar instead of honey.

MAKE IT GLUTEN-FREE

Use a gluten-free flour.

WHAT TO DO WITH LEFTOVERS

The great thing with Greek sweets that do not require refrigeration like this recipe is that they last for a long time. They will keep for at least a couple of months after making as long as you keep them in a sealed container. They make a wonderful accompaniment to your morning coffee or end-of-the-night cup of tea.

COURAGE

I was drawn to the kitchen even as a boy.

Outside the kitchen I saw a world that I didn't want to be part of. It was a world just of men – uncles and cousins who would sit outside at family gatherings drinking, while the women were inside the kitchen doing the hard work, cooking, washing and cleaning.

Something just felt wrong about this. Even as a little boy, I knew it wasn't fair for the women to do the cooking and hard domestic labour while the men just sat outside drinking. Inside the kitchen I found a whole different world. One where the energy and safety of women made me feel safe and seen.

This gendered division of labour limits us so deeply as men. The traditional idea of the kitchen not being the domain of men has a deeply negative impact. It signals to us that our role is not to care in ways that are soft, nurturing and emotional. Also implied is that women are somehow less than us, that this is 'women's work' to serve men.

There is something so tender about making a meal for someone you care about. Its intimacy is in the act of sharing without expectation of reciprocity, just so your meal may provide succour to soothe a hard day and make the person feel valued and cared for.

I learnt to cook at a young age. My first memories of cooking are from when I was about 6 or 7. I was a very awkward young boy and adolescent, with very low self-esteem, a by-product of a childhood marred by racism and bullying. Home was a challenging space, as my parents' deep love for my sister and

Give me a lever long enough and a fulcrum on which to place it, and I shall move the world.

– ARCHIMEDES

I was interwoven with their own conflict, trauma and unhappiness, which made me seek comfort and escape in food. Those years of being bullied at school left an imprint on me that made me feel unsafe around most other boys and men.

Trying to work through this was a lonely journey. I felt ugly, hairy and lumpy, and that I wasn't like the other boys in the country town of Mt Beauty, where I grew up. There were no other boys I could speak to, so I naturally assumed there was something wrong with me, something broken in me that I just did not know how to fix.

I was also without the emotional intelligence and tools to communicate my needs. As I discussed earlier, I grew up in a home where love was shown through acts of sacrifice, not words or affection. I struggled to make friends, to muster the confidence to think people would want to know me and like me.

What I did know how to do was cook, and inviting small groups of people over for a meal became a safe way for me to make new friendships. In that kitchen I felt confident and assured, like I finally had a language I could speak to show people who I was. When I found myself busy enjoying a meal together with others, there was no oxygen in the room left to feed my anxieties and insecurities. I want anyone identifying as a boy or a man to be able to embrace this part of themselves, too. It can be life-changing and life-saving.

Food has always been deeply connected to love in my family. It has often been the language to fill the void that intergenerational trauma bestows on you. Touch, hugs and the words 'I love you' were like an ancient lost language that none of us knew how to speak growing up. What we did know was love through action. And this is where the power of food and sacrifice came into it.

Food should be one of our most pure forms of pleasure, and it is, yet it's complicated at times too. Good food nourishes and connects us, brings us joy, good health, laughter and the deepest connections with our bodies and with others. Food can traverse any barriers, language or otherwise, as it's a door to our shared humanity.

Yet food for me has also been a place of great shame, an anaesthetic to numb hurt and loneliness in my life and a way to punish myself, too. In truth, how could I write a cookbook without being honest about how vulnerable it made me feel? I couldn't. I started writing this cookbook at a time when I had never felt more disconnected from my body; I felt like a stranger within it. I was the heaviest I had ever been in my life and felt alone in my own body. The last thing I wanted to do was write about the joy of cooking and food when in recent times it had been a sanctuary for my sadness.

My relationship with food has always been deeply complex for me; it is both a place of pleasure and punishment, connection and loneliness. I grew up feeling so ugly, worthless and unlovable in my body and my self and looked for ways to be invisible. As men we don't have many safe spaces to talk about body image and our self-esteem.

I have used writing this cookbook as a form of therapy for me. To ask myself what kind of relationship I want to have with food and, most importantly, with myself.

As I have written each recipe, I have made it a chance to re-imagine my relationship with food and ask myself again what is the void it seeks to fill for me? What is the love it seeks to make amends for and the hurt it seeks to numb? These are questions I have grappled with all my life.

I think, in essence, that food offers an unconditional acceptance of yourself; in that moment it allows you to be as you feel without apology or judgement. Food does not judge you; we are the ones who place a judgement on ourselves for whatever we eat. We make it about weakness or strength, discipline or sloth, beauty or ugliness, laziness or strength, acceptance or rejection.

In this book are the recipes I make when love and compassion for myself are at their strongest. These are the recipes that make me feel at home, whatever I am going through.

In documenting these recipes and sharing my love of cooking and food with you, it has helped me too. I have been unpacking what lies at the heart of this. Intergenerational trauma carries its own scars and it makes sense that food can be a balm that soothes it. It is also an act of self-care, enabling me to survive moments in my life that would otherwise have been intolerable.

In re-authoring this narrative, I have returned to cooking with an awareness that it's something for me to enjoy and experience without judgement and shame, that my body needs nurturing and energy to enable me to be all I can be.

This has allowed me to reconnect with my culture and food from a place of acceptance and compassion. To find alternative ways that are about eating from a place of nourishment rather than overeating to grapple with anxiety, stress and loneliness. I am not going to pretend I won't still struggle at times, but I feel more aware of what is at the heart of this and have the awareness to better navigate it. I also remind myself that there may be times when I need food as a form of comfort, too – no judgement, no failure and no shame, just me being kind to me.

If you can relate to any of this and are working on the same issues, know as always you are enough and perfect as you are. You are seen and loved. Be kind and to yourself. Now, more than ever, we need more love, forgiveness and tenderness for ourselves.

Κουλουράκια

Koulourakia | Sesame cookies

SERVES 10 TO 12

500 g (1 lb 2 oz) unsalted
  butter, softened
220 g (8 oz/1 cup) white
  (granulated) sugar
250 ml (8½ fl oz/1 cup)
  lukewarm milk
8 medium eggs, separated
25 g (1 oz) vanilla sugar
zest of ½ lemon
zest of 1 orange
1 teaspoon ammonia baking
  powder
1.5 kg (3 lb 5 oz) self-raising
  (self-rising) flour, plus extra
  for dusting
extra 2 egg yolks, beaten
1 tablespoon water
sesame seeds, for sprinkling
  (optional)

These remind me of Greek Easter and family gatherings, as these are Easter biscuits (though they can be enjoyed any time of year). They remind me of coming back from midnight service at the local Greek church with our candles lit, desperately trying to make it home without the flames going out.

We sit with our beautifully dyed red eggs (representing the blood of Christ) and take turns in seeing who can crack the others in egg fights (the cracking of the egg symbolises Christ's resurrection). We would do this while enjoying our avgolemono soup with some delicious sweet Greek Easter bread called tsoureki. In Greece, egg cracking, or *tsougrisma*, begins after the holy Saturday, as the First Resurrection, and finishes with a Greek feast at my mum's on the Sunday.

Cream the butter and sugar in a stand mixer on medium speed until smooth. Add milk, egg yolks, vanilla, sugar, lemon zest and orange zest and mix on medium speed for 5 minutes.

In a separate clean bowl, mix the egg whites for about 5 minutes until they are stiff, like you are making a meringue. Fold the egg white mixture into the butter mixture.

Gradually add flour and ammonia, mixing on low speed until you get a thick but soft dough (add more flour if you need to).

Turn out dough onto a lightly floured surface and knead for about 5 minutes – you want it not to stick to your fingers but not be hard or dry so it might crack (only add a little flour at a time if needed, as you don't want to make the dough difficult to knead and roll).

Cover with a clean tea towel and leave to rest for 30 minutes.

Cut small pieces (about the size of a walnut in its shell) and gently roll them out with your fingers, like a thin cigar (remember they will rise significantly in the oven), and then form them into any shape you like (as pictured).

Preheat the oven to 180°C (360°F) and line at least 2 baking trays (more if needed, depending on the size of your trays) with baking paper. Combine extra egg yolks with water and brush each of the dough pieces. Top with sesame seeds, if you like (see tip on page 209). Bake for 20–30 minutes until golden, then set aside to cool.

MAKE IT VEGAN

Replace the eggs with a vegan egg mix or leave out altogether, use a vegan milk like soy or almond milk and vegan butter.

MAKE IT GLUTEN-FREE

Use gluten-free flour.

WHAT TO DO WITH LEFTOVERS

The great thing with Greek sweets like this that do not require refrigeration is that they last safely for a couple of months as long as you keep them in a sealed container.

Κουραμπιέδες

Kourabiedes | Shortbreads

MAKES ABOUT 35 BISCUITS

250 g (9 oz/2 cups) slivered
   almonds
500 g (1 lb 2 oz) unsalted
   butter, at room
   temperature
3 tablespoons icing
   (confectioners') sugar
3 egg yolks
30 ml (1 fl oz) ouzo
1 teaspoon lemon zest
1 teaspoon vanilla sugar
100 g (3½ oz/⅔ cup) plain
   (all-purpose) flour, plus
   extra for dusting
300 g (10½ oz/2 cups) self-
   raising (self-rising) flour
extra 300 g (10½ oz) icing
   (confectioners') sugar, plus
   extra for sprinkling
125 ml (4 fl oz/½ cup)
   rosewater

This sweet is my dear friend Heidi's favourite sweet – she simply cannot get enough of the irresistible combination of icing sugar topping and biscuit filled with almonds, rosewater and ouzo. She will let out the biggest belly laugh and smile as she enjoys these little bites of deliciousness.

Preheat the oven to 150°C (300°F).

Line a baking tray with baking paper and spread with almonds. Cook for about 10–15 minutes, or until golden and toasted. Set aside to cool.

Put butter in the bowl of a stand mixer and beat on high until fluffy. Add the icing sugar and egg yolks and beat on high speed for 5–10 minutes until it triples in volume and reaches a nice fluffy consistency.

Add the ouzo, lemon zest and vanilla sugar and continue to mix for 1 minute on low speed.

Add the almonds and mix on low speed for a further minute.

Sift both flours into the mixture while mixing at low speed, and once fully combined, stop mixing. Put the dough hook onto your stand mixer and mix on low speed for 1 minute. If you do not have a stand mixer, you can do all of this with a hand mixer.

Turn out the dough onto a lightly floured bench. Knead the dough for 2–3 minutes until it's smooth and soft.

Cover with a clean tea towel and set aside for 10 minutes to rest.

Increase the oven temperature to 180°C (360°F) and line 2 baking trays with baking paper. Cut the dough into small pieces and shape into small half-moon shapes with your hands (as pictured – though you can even cut it with a cup or use cookie cutters of any shape, especially if cooking with children, but they are traditionally a half-moon shape).

Place dough shapes on prepared trays, allowing enough room for them to spread. Bake for 30 minutes, or until they are a nice golden colour. Set aside on a baking tray for 5 minutes to cool and spray or sprinkle with the rosewater over them.

Spread 100 g (3½ oz) of the icing sugar on a baking tray. Gently place biscuits on top of the icing sugar.

Sift the remaining icing sugar over the top to cover the biscuits completely.

Take them one by one, very carefully so as not to break them, and place them apart on a clean bench. If any part of the biscuit does not have icing sugar, sift more onto those areas. Leave until they cool completely, then place them on a plate to enjoy.

MAKE IT VEGAN

By using vegan butter and replacing the eggs with additional vegan butter to bind.

MAKE IT GLUTEN-FREE

Use gluten-free flour.

WHAT TO DO WITH LEFTOVERS

The great thing about Greek sweets that do not require refrigeration, like these biscuits, is that they last for a long time. They will easily be safe to eat for at least a couple of months after making as long as you keep them in a sealed container. A wonderful accompaniment to your morning coffee or end-of-night cup of tea.

Παστέλι

Pasteli | Sesame bars

SERVES 10 TO 12

620 g (1 lb 6 oz/4 cups)
  sesame seeds
350 g (12½ oz/1 cup) honey
3 teaspoons white
  (granulated) sugar
2 teaspoons cold water
1 teaspoon lemon juice
250 g (9 oz/2 cups) slivered
  almonds

Pasteli is made from just two ingredients, honey and sesame seeds. The Ancient Greeks had a very similar recipe, using honey and different nuts. These highly nutritious snacks were typically consumed during times of traditional Greek Orthodox fasting known as Nistia. It was even referred to in Homer's Iliad as a favourite with warriors.

Preheat the oven to 140°C (285°F). Line 2 baking trays with baking paper.

Spread the sesame seeds on one and the almonds on the other and bake for about 30 minutes, turning every 3–5 minutes until golden.

If you are short on time, you can also toast the sesame seeds and almonds in a frying pan over a low heat for about 10 minutes until golden brown.

Combine the honey, sugar, water and a few drops of lemon juice in a pot over a medium heat and bring to the boil. Remove from heat immediately and scoop out any white from the honey.

Combine the toasted sesame seeds and almonds in a large frying pan over a low heat and, while still hot, pour in the honey syrup mixture and stir to combine. Cook for a couple of minutes, or until the syrup starts to thicken.

Working quickly so the mixture doesn't set, transfer mixture to a large chopping board and spread it out with the back of a wet tablespoon. Using a rolling pin, roll the mixture out to a rectangle about 30 cm (12 in) × 10 cm (4 in) and about 1–2 cm (½ in) thickness (depends on how thick you like it).

Place plastic wrap all over the sesame spread (lightly wet the top of the spread with cold water first just using your hands) and roll out flat with the rolling pin.

Smooth the sides, using a butter knife, while it is still hot. Use a ruler to cut pieces before it sets and hardens. Cut at a 45-degree angle to create diamond shapes (you can cut into any shape and size you like though, the key is to do it before the sesame seed hardens and is no longer malleable – you have about a 10-minute window to do this). Set aside to cool, and enjoy!

MAKE IT VEGAN

By using maple, date or dandelion syrup, vegan honey or agave nectar instead of honey.

MAKE IT GLUTEN-FREE

It already is!

WHAT TO DO WITH LEFTOVERS

Store in an airtight sealed container and they will keep well for 1–2 months without refrigeration needed.

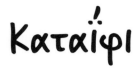

Kataifi | Sweet shredded pastries

SERVES 10 TO 12

750 g (1 lb 11 oz) kataifi
    phyllo
300 g (10½ oz) walnuts,
    lightly crushed
1 teaspoon ground cinnamon
1 teaspoon breadcrumbs
½ teaspoon freshly grated
    nutmeg
1 teaspoon white (granulated)
    sugar
500 g (1 lb 2 oz) butter,
    melted
50 g (1¾ oz) pistachios,
    crushed

SYRUP

660 g (1 lb 7 oz/3 cups) white
    (granulated) sugar
750 ml (25½ fl oz/2½ cups)
    water
1 tablespoon lemon juice
½ lemon zest
1 cinnamon stick

I love working with this pastry as it is so unique, like long locks of hair magically turned into pastry. It feels unique to touch, stretch and roll with. Working with it can take some practice, but have fun with it! It looks fragile but it's actually very robust. If it breaks, no worries, just grab some more strands to fill any holes.

If you have bought kataifi from the freezer section of a shop, make sure to place it in your fridge the night before to thaw out. Then take the pastry out of the fridge the day you are using it and let it sit in its packet for 2 hours at room temperature before opening it to get it to room temperature (it will be much easier to work this way).

Using your fingers, gently tear apart the pastry to make it fluffy and spread it out as much as you can without tearing it too much. Imagine you are trying to untangle knots in long hair.

Combine walnuts, ground cinnamon, breadcrumbs, nutmeg and sugar in a small bowl.

Pull the pastry apart into 12–14 equal pieces. You are likely to need to pull its threads apart to make it into the shapes you want, but it doesn't matter if you do tear it. Now take a few of the phyllo threads and place them together to make a long strip of about 30 cm (12 in) long × 10cm (4 in) wide. Overlap any threads that have torn and flatten the pastry with your hands.

Cover pieces with a damp towel as you go so phyllo does not dry out.

Grease a baking tray with melted butter and preheat the oven to 180°C (360°F).

Place a teaspoonful of the walnut mixture into the centre of each of the phyllo parcels and roll into a cigar shape, using your fingers to close in the ends to contain the mixture. Transfer to the prepared tray, snuggling them next to each other so they do not move and won't expand when cooking. This is important so that they hold their shape.

Drizzle parcels with melted butter. Reduce oven temperature to 170°C (340°F). Place parcels on the bottom rack of the oven and cook for about 1 hour and 15 minutes, or until crisp and golden.

About 15 minutes before the end of the cooking time, prepare the syrup. Combine sugar, water, lemon juice, zest and cinnamon stick in a saucepan over a medium heat and cook for about 5–6 minutes, or until mixture is bubbling and hot.

Pour hot syrup all over the kataifi parcels.

Set aside in a cool, dry place (not in the fridge) to soak overnight.

Sprinkle with crushed pistachios to serve.

MAKE IT VEGAN

By using a vegan butter.

MAKE IT GLUTEN-FREE

By using a gluten-free phyllo.

WHAT TO DO WITH LEFTOVERS

Refrigerate in an airtight container and safely enjoy for another two weeks.

Δίπλες (με τον τρόπο της Καλαμάτας)

Diples (Kalamata style) | Deep-fried pastries

SERVES 10 TO 12

150 g (5½ oz) walnuts
1 teaspoon cinnamon
3 eggs, separated
1 teaspoon vanilla sugar
2 teaspoons sugar
pinch of salt
300 g (10½ oz/2 cups) special white flour/farina flour or 00 plain flour, plus extra for dusting
1 teaspoon baking powder
1 litre (34 fl oz) canola oil

SYRUP
300 g (10½ oz) honey
60 ml (2 fl oz/¼ cup) water

If you ever want to get my mum, Sia, talking about her daughter Nola's wedding, bring up the topic of diples. She made hundreds of these honeyed Greek pastries for my sister's wedding, which was a true act of love, because they can be challenging to make! Once you master them, though, the sweetness of the honey and the crack of the pastry with the chopped walnuts is an irresistible combo and they're well worth the effort. For my mum, making this dish is an expression of love and pride, because the care and time that goes into making them is something you would only do for a loved one.

The easiest way to make these is using a pasta machine, but you can also do it without it (though it is trickier). If doing it by hand, the key is to roll out each of the pastry sheets multiple times to stretch and thin it out.

Pick a large serving platter to plate the diples on for when they are ready. We traditionally like to stack them on top of each other, layer by layer, creating a triangle-like formation.

Crush the walnuts in a mortar and pestle or small hand mixer. Combine with cinnamon and set aside.

Beat the egg yolks with vanilla sugar and sugar in a bowl until well combined.

In a separate bowl, beat the egg whites with a pinch of salt and a few drops of cold water until stiff, like you are making a meringue.

Add the egg yolk mixture to the egg white mixture and mix to combine. Beat for 2 minutes, using a whisk or hand mixer.

Gradually sift in the flour and baking powder and mix for about 5 minutes to form a firm dough.

Turn out dough onto a floured bench and knead with your knuckles to create a firm dough.

If you are using a pasta machine, cut a small piece from the dough similar to a sheet of lasagne. Thread it through the pasta machine 3 times, each time on a finer setting, starting with level 3, then level 4, then level 7, until you get a thin sheet of pastry.

Remember dough has to be firm, otherwise it will stick to the pasta machine.

If you do not have a pasta machine, you can roll the pastry out with a rolling pin until very fine, then using your fingers, pull the edges of the sheet as far as you can without tearing them. On a flat surface, cut sheets from the pastry, using scissors or a knife, into rectangular pieces of about 12 cm/4¾ in × 25 cm/10 in.

Heat the canola oil in a small pot until hot.

Working one at a time, drop each sheet of pastry into the oil and wait until the dough starts to bubble. Using two forks, roll the pastry in the oil to form a log shape (taking care not to burn yourself!) and fry each for about 1 minute until lightly golden. Transfer to a plate lined with a paper towel to drain excess oil, then place on baking trays.

Prepare the syrup. Combine honey and water in a medium-sized pot over a medium heat and bring to the boil (takes about 5 minutes), then reduce heat to low and take off straight away. Now take one diples at a time and hold it over the pot of syrup. Spoon 3 tablespoons of the syrup over each diples and 2 tablespoons of the syrup on the inside of each. Hold it for a few seconds over the pot to let any excess syrup drip back into it.

Layer on a serving platter and sprinkle generously with the walnut and cinnamon mixture.

MAKE IT VEGAN

By using maple, date or dandelion syrup, vegan honey or agave nectar instead of honey.

MAKE IT GLUTEN-FREE

Use a gluten-free flour.

WHAT TO DO WITH LEFTOVERS

These will keep well in an airtight container for a month and do not need refrigeration.

Χαλβάς

Halva | Semolina pudding

SERVES 10 TO 12

1 litre (34 fl oz/4 cups) water
110 g (4 oz/½ cup) sugar
juice and coarse zest of
    ½ lemon
250 ml (8½ fl oz/1 cup)
    canola oil
125 g (4½ oz/1 cup) fine
    semolina
165 g (6 oz/1 cup) coarse
    semolina
125 g (4½ oz/1 cup) slivered
    almonds
1 teaspoon ground cinnamon,
    plus extra to serve
1 small stick cinnamon
almond flakes, to serve

MAKE IT VEGAN

It already is!

MAKE IT GLUTEN-FREE

By using a gluten-free semolina such
as rice semolina.

WHAT TO DO WITH LEFTOVERS

Refrigerate and keep covered in
plastic wrap and they will safely last
for another month.

To my mum's great annoyance, when she goes vegan for the
Great Lent leading up to Easter, I often tease her about the
fact that I started way ahead of her in cutting out meats and
fish and, as a vegetarian, I am more devout than she is. There
are multiple versions of halva that include everything from
almonds and pistachios to non-vegan versions with chocolate
and cheese.

Cook the water, sugar, lemon juice, lemon zest and cinnamon stick
in a large saucepan over a medium heat for about 5 minutes, or
until the sugar is absorbed and the mixture comes to the boil.
Reduce to a simmer and cook for 2–3 minutes, then remove
from heat and set aside.

Spread almonds on a baking tray lined with baking paper and
bake for about 5 minutes, or until golden, and set aside.

Heat oil in another large pot or saucepan over a medium heat
until hot, then reduce heat to low and gradually pour in both the
fine and coarse semolina, continuously stirring with a wooden
spoon, cooking for 6–8 minutes, or until a deep golden colour
(keep stirring or it will burn).

Stir in toasted almonds, reserving some to garnish, and ground
cinnamon and stir through a few times before removing from the
heat. Using a ladle, carefully and gradually pour the syrup mixture
into the semolina mixture (taking care not to burn yourself, as
the semolina mixture will bubble up). Once all the syrup has
been added in, stir with a wooden spoon until mixture is thick
and combined.

Remove lemon zest and cinnamon stick from the mix with a fork.

While still hot, pour immediately into your cake mould (you do not
need to grease the lining, mixture can go straight in). You can do
one large cake mould or a series of small ones.

Make sure the halva surface is smooth and flat by using a spoon
or knife to smooth out.

Set aside to cool for 45 minutes, then turn out onto a plate
and sprinkle with ground cinnamon and reserved almond flakes
to serve.

Μπακλαβάς

Baklava

SERVES 10 TO 12

300 g (10½ oz) unsalted
  butter
375 g (13 oz) phyllo
  pastry (about
  18–22 sheets)
500 g (1 lb 2 oz) walnuts,
  chopped (or a mix of
  walnuts, pistachios
  and almonds)
2 teaspoons cinnamon
  powder
2 teaspoons ground cloves
whole cloves, to serve
  (optional)

SYRUP
600 g (1 lb 5 oz) white
  (granulated) sugar
400 ml (13½ fl oz) water
zest of 1 lemon or orange
2 cloves
1 cinnamon stick
80 g (2¾ oz) honey

MAKE IT VEGAN

By using maple, date or dandelion
syrup, vegan honey or agave nectar
instead of honey.

MAKE IT GLUTEN-FREE

Use a gluten-free phyllo pastry.

WHAT TO DO WITH LEFTOVERS

Store in an airtight container and
refrigerate and you can still enjoy for
the next couple of weeks.

Who doesn't love baklava?! It is impossible not to be seduced by
buttered layers of phyllo filled with nuts and finished off with
an incredible honey and orange-infused syrup. A Christmas
tradition for all Greeks – even when you think you can't eat any
more, you should always make room for this special dessert.

Melt the butter in a saucepan over a low heat, being careful not
to burn it. Use a cooking brush to butter the bottom and sides
of a baking pan. Layer the sheets of phyllo on the bottom of
the baking dish, one at a time, to form the base, making sure to
sprinkle each one with melted butter. Use about 10–12 layers for
the base.

In a large bowl, mix the chopped nuts, cinnamon and ground
clove together. Sprinkle some of the nut mixture over the phyllo
base. Continue to add phyllo sheets, one at a time, sprinkling
each with melted butter and nut mix. Keep going until you reach
the top, or are down to your last sheet of pastry. Top with the last
phyllo sheet and cover it with plenty of butter.

Preheat the oven to 150°C (300°F). Pop the baklava in the fridge
for 15 minutes. Remove from the fridge and, using a sharp knife,
cut all the way down into pieces. Sprinkle the top with some
cold water.

Place the baklava on the lower rack of the oven and bake for
about 1½ hours, until all the phyllo layers are crisp and golden.

MAKE THE SYRUP

Mix all the ingredients for the syrup (except honey) and bring
to the boil. Boil for about 2 minutes until the sugar is dissolved.
Remove the pan from the heat and stir in the honey, then let the
syrup cool down. As soon as the baklava is ready, slowly ladle
the syrup over the hot baklava, until it is fully absorbed.

Allow the baklava to cool down completely and serve once the
syrup has soaked throughout.

Λουκουμάδες

Loukoumades | Honey balls

SERVES 10 TO 12

25 g (1 oz) wet or dried yeast
½ teaspoon sugar
580 ml (19½ fl oz/2⅓ cups)
   warm water
500 g (1 lb 2 oz) self-raising
   (self-rising) flour

WALNUT MIX
125 g (4½ oz/1 cup) walnuts
1 teaspoon freshly grated or
   ground nutmeg
1 teaspoon ground cinnamon,
   plus extra to serve

HONEY MIX
200 g (7 oz) honey, plus extra
   to serve
80 ml (2½ fl oz/⅓ cup) water
wedge of lemon
1 cinnamon stick
1 litre (34 fl oz) canola oil,
   for frying

MAKE IT VEGAN
By using maple, date or dandelion
syrup, vegan honey or agave nectar
instead of honey.

MAKE IT GLUTEN-FREE
Use gluten-free flour.

WHAT TO DO WITH LEFTOVERS
Store any leftover mixture in a
container and refrigerate and you can
use it within the following 2 days.

These little golden jewels of honeyed, nut-fried goodness
are found everywhere on the streets of Greece, filling the
laneways with the sweet scent of cinnamon and honey. They
are so prized, folklore says, that they were offered as rewards
for the first Olympics in 776 BC, with Greek poet Callimachus
writing that the winners were given honey tokens. These fried
doughnuts are indeed worth their weight in gold.

Combine yeast, sugar and 80 ml (2½ fl oz/⅓ cup) of the warm
water in a large bowl. Cover with plastic wrap and leave for
10 minutes.

Add the flour and remaining warm water and stir with a wooden
spoon to form a thick batter. Cover again with plastic wrap and
set aside for 30 minutes. The mixture should roughly double
in size.

To make the walnut mix, crush the walnuts in a mortar and pestle,
add the nutmeg and cinnamon and stir to combine.

To make the honey mix, combine honey, water, lemon and
cinnamon stick in a pan over a low heat and cook for 5 minutes.
Set aside.

Heat oil in a deep pan or saucepan until hot.

Using your hand, scoop up handfuls of the mixture and squeeze
so it pops out the top of your fist, then use a spoon to flick the
mixture into the hot oil. You can also just drop tablespoons of
the mixture straight into the oil (dip the spoon in cold water as
you go to keep it clean and prevent the mixture from sticking).

Cook in batches of 5 or 6 at a time for about 3 minutes, or until
golden brown, using a slotted spoon to toss them in the oil.
Once cooked, transfer to a plate lined with a paper towel to
drain excess oil.

Transfer to a serving platter, drizzle over the honey mix and then
finish with the walnut mix and extra honey and cinnamon to serve.

Ελληνικός καφές

Greek coffee, three ways

SERVES 1

Greek coffee is intrinsically part of our daily life. Since 1475, the Greek kafenio (coffee shop) has been a place of gathering, not simply to enjoy a coffee but to connect, make new friendships and have passionate conversations about politics and sports. It remains a place where all Greeks can gather as a place of social inclusion despite tough economic times.

The Greek coffee experience is unique in so many ways. Firstly, it is traditionally made in a briki, which is like a small bronze coffee pot (you can buy them online or from Mediterranean supermarkets). Secondly, the coffee and sugar (if added) are placed in the briki together before water is added, rather than being added later. Thirdly, we want a kaimaki (froth) on top of our coffee. That's the sign of a well-made coffee and it covers all of the coffee (which is served in an espresso-sized cup). And finally, Greek coffee can offer you an insight into your entire future via a reading by fortunetellers (or aunts). Once you've drunk your coffee, the cup is turned over onto its saucer and the pattern left in the cup will tell you what awaits you in your future!

Sketos

1 teaspoon Greek coffee
250 ml (8½ fl oz/1 cup) water

If you like your coffee strong, thick and bitter, sketos is the way to go. This is Greek coffee with no sugar at all.

Metrios

1 teaspoon Greek coffee
1 teaspoon sugar
250 ml (8½ fl oz/1 cup) water

The way most Greeks enjoy their coffee is metrios, which is where you make the coffee with one teaspoon of sugar for each cup of coffee you make. It's not too sweet and not too bitter, just right.

Glykos

1 teaspoon Greek coffee
2 teaspoons sugar
250 ml (8½ fl oz/1 cup) water

Now for those of you who have a real sweet tooth, the glykos way is the Greek coffee for you. We are not messing around; this is sweet coffee at its finest.

Add coffee and sugar (if using) to a briki. Add water. Stir over a low heat and bring the mixture to the boil. Remove immediately from the heat as soon as it is bubbling. Pour into Greek coffee cups or an espresso coffee cup.

A tip here: if you are making two coffees at a time, pour half a coffee cup's worth in each cup and then pour again to fill, to ensure both cups get some of the kaimaki.

MAKE IT VEGAN

It already is!

MAKE IT GLUTEN-FREE

It already is!

WHAT TO DO WITH LEFTOVERS

Keep in the fridge and use to make a frappe (iced coffee).

Φραπέ

Frappe

SERVES 1

GLYKOS (SWEET)

2 teaspoons Nescafé instant
coffee

2 teaspoons sugar

3 tablespoons cold water,
plus 125 ml (4 fl oz/½ cup)
cold water

2 large ice cubes

2 tablespoons vanilla ice
cream (optional)

⅛ teaspoon ground cinnamon

METRIOS (MEDIUM)

2 teaspoons Nescafé instant
coffee

1 teaspoon sugar

3 tablespoons cold water,
plus 125 ml (4 fl oz/½ cup)
cold water

250 ml (8½ fl oz/1 cup
full-cream (whole) milk

2 large ice cubes

2 tablespoons vanilla ice cream
(optional)

⅛ teaspoon ground cinnamon

SKETOS (PLAIN, NO SUGAR)

2 teaspoons Nescafé instant
coffee

3 tablespoons cold water,
plus 125 ml (4 fl oz/½ cup)
cold water

2 large ice cubes

2 tablespoons vanilla ice cream
(optional)

⅛ teaspoon ground cinnamon

MAKE IT VEGAN

Use soy, almond or oat milk and
vegan ice cream.

MAKE IT GLUTEN-FREE

It already is!

Frappe (Greek iced coffee) is everywhere in summertime Greece. You won't find a cafe table without one, as it has been the nation's most popular coffee drink for more than four decades. It is intrinsically part of our outdoor cafe coffee culture that travellers from around the world adore too. The Greek version of it is a frothy iced coffee made with coffee, sugar, water, ice cubes and sometimes milk. Like Greek coffee, frappe comes in four typical styles, determined by the amount of sugar you add.

The easiest way to make a frappe is with a frappe mixer (you can buy one cheaply online – they are usually called a milk frother/hand-held blender or foam maker), otherwise you can use a regular cocktail shaker or a milkshake machine.

Add instant coffee, sugar (if you are using any) and 3 tablespoons cold water to a tall glass.

Either whiz the mixture with your hand-held blender straight into the glass or pour into your cocktail shaker or milkshake maker to shake or blend until you get a brown, thick creamy foam. Slowly pour in the rest of the water and gently stir it through. Add milk (if using) and stir, then add the ice cubes. Add ice cream (if using) and finish by sprinkling the cinnamon on top.

Add or subtract ice cubes and ice cream to suit the size of your glass.

Greek
Wisdom

Sia's kitchen wisdom

I have learnt almost everything about cooking from my mum, Sia. To thrive in the kitchen, you need a respect for the food that you cook with. Grow what you can, as it tastes better and is healthier for you. Use what you have rather than buy more. Take care and don't rush in the kitchen when cooking, and be generous with the ingredients that you have.

SIA'S TOP COOKING TIPS

- Food needs love and patience. Without this, 'the food does not come nice'.

- Be patient with yourself when it comes to cooking. Don't worry if it doesn't turn out how you hoped the first time you try a recipe. No one is born knowing it all – just know that practice is everything and next time will be better!

- Taste and season as you go – always start with less seasoning, as you can add more salt, pepper, herbs and garlic as you go. Take care with salt, adding little amounts at a time, as the one thing you cannot save a meal from is too much salt.

- If you've accidentally burnt the food you're cooking, immediately transfer the food to a fresh pot or pan with fresh oil. Otherwise you will be left with a burnt flavour in your dish.

- Frying anything in a batter will often dirty your oil. Change your oil and wipe your pan halfway through to keep your food clean.

- Work with low or medium heat at all times, except when you need to get something to boil or are deep frying. Food tastes better when it is cooked with patience.

- A spoonful of flour can save a soup that just won't thicken. Add it, but make sure to dissolve it with a little bit of warm water in a cup before pouring it in.

- If frying up vegetable patties and they are not holding, get a plate of plain flour and gently pat them on both sides in the flour, then fry. This will help hold them together.

Wisdom outweighs any wealth.
– SOPHOCLES

- If you're making lathera-style casseroles (cooking in lots of olive oil), do not stir after you have added all the ingredients. You will break up the vegetables and ruin the dish. Gently shake the pan and be patient.

- Save a lumpy béchamel sauce by adding more milk and stirring constantly over a low heat with a wooden spoon. If it is still too lumpy, pass through a sieve and continue to stir.

- When roasting or frying vegetables together, do it in the order of the time they will take to fry to ensure evenly cooked food. From first to last: pumpkin (winter squash), potatoes, sweet potatoes, carrots, green beans, capsicum (bell pepper), cauliflower, eggplant (aubergine), zucchini (courgette), brussels sprouts, spinach, silverbeet (Swiss chard), broad beans, mushrooms, mint, parsley, dill, basil.

- Don't forget many vegetables, such as eggplants (aubergines) and zucchinis (courgettes), release natural water and juices that will help cook your fabulous vegetable casserole. Don't overdo it with canned tomatoes or water.

- When boiling any beans, don't add salt till the very end (in the last 5 minutes of cooking the dish), as salt will stop the beans from properly cooking.

- When using fresh herbs in a dish, add them at the very end so that you get the full fresh flavours of the herb (the last 5–10 minutes).

- When baking potatoes in the oven, always add a cup of water to the roasting dish to prevent them from burning.

- Don't be afraid of food getting a good colour. Potatoes, yemista, pastitso and moussaka are meant to be golden. If there is no colour, they are undercooked.

- When cooking with okra, rinse first with vinegar then cover with a tea towel and place in the sun for up to 3 hours. This adds flavour and prevents them becoming too mushy when cooked.

Sia's 'waste nothing, use everything' guide to cooking

For generations in my family, wasting nothing and using everything you had was a way of life, born originally from poverty and circumstance. Meat was a luxury. A vegetarian and vegan diet was commonplace.

My great grandmother Georgia had to travel on foot for many miles just to buy rice, pasta, flour and sugar. It was a costly journey and these items were a luxury and bought in bulk. Ensuring they lasted as long as possible was critical.

In all things
of nature, there is
something marvellous.
– ARISTOTLE

SIA'S TOP TIPS FOR REDUCING FOOD WASTE

- Use every part of the vegetable – waste nothing. Those leftover, and often discarded, bits of carrot, onion, celery, fennel and the stems of any fresh herbs all make for perfect ingredients for a vegan stock; just add salt, pepper and water. Also, you can put the stems of dill, basil, parsley or mint into olive oil and leave for a few hours and you have flavoured oil for your salads. Same with leftover garlic for your cooking oils.

- When vegetables such as eggplant (aubergine), zucchini (courgette), pumpkin (winter squash), carrots or beetroot (beets) have nearly gone bad, don't throw them away. They are perfect to use for mezze. Slice any rough parts off, then slice thinly and toss with a little olive oil before grilling. You can then toss with a little vinegar, parsley, garlic and olive oil and use for platters or sandwiches.

- If you have tomatoes on the turn, slice any black bits off, then blanch and, once cool, peel. Grate the flesh into a zip-lock bag and freeze for up to a year. Defrost to use in soups and sauces.

- You can also pickle any vegetables nearing their use by date, such as cauliflower, capsicum (bell pepper) or beans. Add to sterilised jars with flavourings such as garlic, salt and herbs, then fill the jars with half boiling water and half white vinegar. Top with canola oil and seal.

- Instead of throwing away the leaves of a beetroot (beet) or stems of silverbeet (Swiss chard) just boil them until tender and dress them with olive oil, lemon, salt and pepper.

- Fresh herbs in abundance can be preserved for use when they're out of season. Herbs such as mint, dill and parsley can be finely chopped and placed into freezer bags.

- You can also prolong fresh herbs by drying them for use. With herbs like fresh mint, sage, rosemary, thyme and bay leaves, place them on a towel and dry them in the sun. Next place them in a blender or crush with your hands and place in an airtight jar, and you have dried herbs for the next year.

- A couple of potatoes added to your fruit bowl will extend the life of your apples.

- After opening a tomato paste jar, cover the top with olive oil to prevent mould from forming when storing in the refrigerator.

- When you just need a few drops of lemon juice, prick the lemon with a fork to squeeze out a few drops.

- Prolong the lifetime of flour, rice and spaghetti by adding a bay leaf to the container to avoid moths forming in the containers.

- In hot months, place your semolina, polenta, breadcrumbs and sesame seeds in your freezer to extend their shelf life. You will still be able to use them in an instant.

- Wherever possible, propagate your vegetables and herbs to grow more produce. For example, if you buy a punnet of basil, don't throw the base away, but plant it firmly into the soil and the basil will regrow. You can also plant your leftover garlic (still in its skin) with the pointy part facing upwards. Cover it in soil and it will grow more garlic.

Sia's guide for leftovers

My mum's family were poor and they survived by growing, selling and bartering what they could. She has a deep respect for the value of food and how not to waste it. I am the same as a result, never wasting leftovers, as I know how lucky I am to have food security. Here are some simple tips from my mum on how to make delicious new dishes from your leftovers.

Potatoes

Transform leftover fries into a potato omelette. Finely slice leftover fries, place in a frying pan and pour over beaten eggs, with feta and any fresh herbs.

You can also take leftover potatoes and make them into a Greek mash potato (see page 144).

Pasta

Use leftover pasta to make a delicious pasta bake. Just toss leftover cooked pasta with any of your favourite chopped herbs and lots of grated cheese and place in a baking dish. Top with a béchamel or tomato sauce and bake until golden.

Soup

Repurpose leftover soups, such as lentil soups, into yummy burgers by draining the liquid and adding eggs, fresh chopped herbs, grated cheese, flour and breadcrumbs to thicken and form into patties.

If you have leftovers from a bean soup, you can drain the liquid and reserve the bean mixture to make into a dip. Add olive oil, lemon, fresh herbs, salt and pepper and blend.

Dough

If you have leftover dough from baking a dish, roll it out into small pita-size breads and fry them in a pan with canola oil until golden. Crumble some Greek feta and oregano all over and roll up and eat while warm.

You can also cut up your leftover dough and freeze it to use later.

Rice

When you have leftover rice from the yemista recipe (page 141), place in a pot with a cup of water and cook it up into a nice pilaf. Leftover cooked rice is great for using in patties – add chopped onion, whisked egg and breadcrumbs, then mix to combine, and form into patties and fry.

Vegetable juices

Never waste the delicious juices at the bottom of your roasted vegetables, potatoes or casseroles; they are liquid gold. Instead, toss some pre-cooked or canned beans like cannellini, northern beans or chickpeas into the juices and roast with olive oil and salt and pepper. Or toast some bread, dip it into the juices and then crumble feta and oregano over it for a delicious snack.

Not what we have but what we enjoy constitutes our abundance.

– EPICURUS

Sia's guide to measurements

My mum's guide to measuring is 'me to mati' – with the eye, by the way something looks or tastes or smells.

Cooking with the eye is a way of cooking from the heart and not from a set of instructions. It's about trusting your senses and being guided by your intuition and instincts. At first, this may feel daunting, but the more you give yourself the freedom to cook this way and to trust yourself, the more it will eventually become like second nature to you.

My mum has mastered this skill over the course of 60 years of cooking. It cannot be taught but it can be learned by anyone. It is learned through the act of sharing a meal together with your loved ones time and time again. This is how I learned to cook and how you can too.

Cooking without following strict measurements and guides is about making the food you love, not what someone has prescribed to you. As my mum told me: 'You have to love what you are doing, and cooking is love for your family and your children and grandchildren. Cooking is love, it is one's imagination, that is my conclusion.'

My mum tells me it's not about making everything you cook perfect; there is no such thing. It's about trusting yourself to cook this way so that the meal itself is an act of pleasure and exploration for you. It is about embracing what you enjoy and love, and trusting your senses to figure it out.

The greater the difficulty, the more the glory in surmounting it.

– EPICURUS

SIA'S MEASURING TIPS

How much flour do you use? 'As much as the dish can take.'

How much olive oil do you use? 'You decide with the mati, I don't want to be swimming in the oil, but there needs to be good enough for what I am cooking.'

How much salt do you use? 'Taste and you will know.'

How much pepper do you use? 'How much you like.'

What do you do if you burn a dish? 'Don't worry, throw it away and start again.'

How many fresh herbs do I use? 'The more herbs the better and it depends what you are cooking.'

When do I know my dough is thick enough? 'You will know with the touch as you go, when it no stick with your fingers you will know it is ready.'

How much garlic do you use? 'How much I like to.'

How long do you cook it for? 'With the eyes and a taste you will know and also it depends on the oven.'

How long do you cook rice for? 'Do not worry, if you cook it too long you can make a pilaf, if you cook it too little you can make soup.'

How do I know a dish I am baking has enough colour? 'If it is nice and golden, that's it!'

What do I do if the flavours don't feel right? 'If something is missing, I add.'

How long do you wash vegetables before cooking? 'You need to wash them three or four times before using, until the water becomes clear.'

Leo's gardening tips

My father, Leo, could grow food and flowers anywhere. I will never forget how he grew this heavenly flower garden in the midst of the barren and brutal asbestos-filled dye wool factory in which he worked in Collingwood for many years. The men would mock him for it; why would he spend his energy clearing debris and spend his own money to create such a garden! My father believed in the power of nature and the beauty of a garden and flowers, and wanted to find it and create it even in the darkest of places. In fact, the darker and harsher the environment, the more important it was to create beauty, in his eyes.

The garden was my father's sanctuary. After a day working in the harshest of jobs in a filthy factory, my father would find his respite in his garden. Here was a place of peace, the solitude allowing him to connect to nature and himself.

My father taught me it is the care and time you take and never the amount you spend. You need to treat plants and vegetables like you would human beings, with care, affection, patience and effort to ensure they will prosper.

LEO'S GARDENING LESSONS

- On very hot days, cover your tomato and cucumber plants with an old bed sheet to protect them from the sun.

- If you are growing seedlings and there is frosty weather coming, cover them with an old bed sheet to protect them from frostbite.

- When you cut your lawn, collect the clippings in a corner of your garden, water them well and leave for a week to dry. They make a great mulch for the base of your tomatoes and will help keep the moisture in your plants.

- Instead of using plastic ties to tie up your tomatoes, cut old pillowcases and clothes into strips. They hold the plants better and allow circulation for them to grow.

- Prune back your olive trees each year to help them grow and produce fruit.

- For best results, always plant eggplants (aubergines) next to basil – they love each other and are in a codependent relationship!

- Eggplants (aubergines), zucchinis (courgettes) and cucumbers are thirsty plants and need to be watered regularly.

- When your zucchini (courgette) plants are not bearing vegetables or flowers, prune them back to give the rest more sun and oxygen to grow.

- Don't plant too many seedlings too closely together in a planter box or garden: like people, they need space to grow. When planting seedlings, make a hole first, fill the hole with a glass of water, then firmly plant.

- Lift up the ground around your seedlings as they grow – this will get more oxygen into the soil, ensuring it doesn't compact and cause disease. When planting seedlings, make sure to separate each one to get the most out of them; don't plant them in clumps.

- Cut the lower branches of your tomato plants, as they usually do not yield fruit and will only suck nutrients from the other parts of the plant. Fertilise the base of your tomato plants with a bit of manure mixed with water, and only water them every second day.

What you leave behind is not what is engraved in stone monuments, but what is woven into the lives of others.

– PERICLES

Ingredient Substitutes

Vegan and dairy-free substitutes

Butter Vegan butter, coconut oil, olive oil or avocado oil

Eggs In savoury dishes, you can substitute eggs with a vegan egg mixture. In sweet dishes where eggs are used for binding, you may be able to substitute eggs with ingredients such as flaxseed egg, chia egg, applesauce, pumpkin (winter squash) puree, mashed banana, baking soda and apple-cider vinegar, silken tofu, plant-based yoghurt, aquafaba (chickpea brine).

Feta Vegan feta is available at most supermarkets. Another alternative is firm tofu – just pat dry with paper towel or a tea towel and marinate overnight in a mixture of water, lemon juice, apple-cider vinegar, Greek oregano and salt.

Honey Any of the following will give you the sweetness of honey: maple syrup, agave nectar, brown rice syrup, barley malt syrup, sorghum syrup, date or dandelion syrup, vegan honey or agave nectar.

Kesari Vegan cheddar or hard cheese

Kefalograviera Vegan hard cheese

Milk Soy, oat or almond milk

Mizithra Vegan parmesan cheese

Ricotta Make your own vegan ricotta (page 13) by substituting full-cream (whole) milk with soy milk.

Yoghurt Greek-style soy yoghurt, plant-based Greek-style yoghurt or Greek-style coconut yoghurt.

One thing I know is that I know nothing. This is the source of my wisdom.
– SOCRATES

Fruit, vegetable and herb substitutes

Basil Mint, parsley, Greek oregano or coriander

Broad beans Butter beans, peas or green beans

Broccoli Brussels sprouts or broccolini

Capsicum (bell pepper) Poblano, anaheim or pimento peppers

Cauliflower Eggplant (aubergine), zucchini (courgette) or carrot

Carrot Sweet potato, pumpkin (winter squash) or potato

Dill Mint, parsley or basil

Eggplant (aubergine) Carrot, potato or cauliflower

Fig Persimmon

Green beans Snake beans, snow peas, string beans or broad beans

Honeydew Watermelon or rockmelon.

Leek Celery or onions.

Lemon Lime, orange juice, apple-cider vinegar or grapefruit juice

Mint Dill, parsley or Greek oregano

Mushroom Eggplant (aubergine), zucchini (courgette), chickpeas or tofu

Onion Spring onions, leek, fennel or celery

Orange Persimmon or mandarin

Parsley Mint, parsley or Greek oregano

Potato Eggplant (aubergine), carrot or sweet potato

Spinach Silverbeet, kale, watercress, bok choy or mustard greens

Silverbeet (Swiss chard) Spinach, vine leaves or sorrel

Vanilla essence Grated lemon zest

Watermelon Rockmelon or honey dew

Wild Greek greens Spinach, chicory or endives

Zucchini (courgette) Eggplant (aubergine), squash, pumpkin (winter squash); in salads, use cucumbers

Even as truth, does error have its lovers.
– PYTHAGORAS

Pasta and grain substitutes

Long-grain rice Jasmine rice, basmati rice, brown rice or medium grain rice

Orzo pasta Penne or ditalini pasta, small elbow macaroni or arborio rice

Ziti pasta Penne, rigatoni or bucatini pasta

Low FODMAP substitutes

It will be good news to IBS sufferers that the Greek diet has many great dishes and ingredients that are low FODMAP, including classics such as saganaki, Greek salad, olives, horta, silverbeet (Swiss chard) and halloumi. As well, the following herbs and spices commonly used in Greek cooking are low FODMAP: basil, bay leaves, cardamom, chilli, cinnamon, cloves, coriander, cumin, fennel seeds, mint, nutmeg, oregano, paprika, parsley, pepper, rosemary, sage, sesame seeds, star anise, tarragon and thyme.

Here is a broad summary of substitutes for some common ingredients that are high FODMAP.

I need to put a very important caveat here: I am not a dietitian or a doctor, rather I have simply done my best to research what foods are low and high FODMAP to try to make this book as inclusive as I can. Please firstly consult your doctor or see a dietitian on such important health matters. This is not medical advice. I cannot recommend highly enough downloading the excellent, science-based Monash University FODMAP diet app to guide you, as it has me. All these alternatives should be eaten in moderation.

Almonds (slivered, whole) Pine nuts or macadamia nuts

Asparagus Green beans or broccolini

Capsicum (bell pepper) With capsicum being high FODMAP, it is best just to substitute with zucchini (courgettes), eggplants (aubergines), potatoes, pumpkin (winter squash) or cauliflower, depending on the recipe.

Flour (wheat) Buckwheat or rice flour

Garlic You can still get the flavour of garlic in your dish by infusing it in olive oil. Peel 6 garlic cloves and place whole in a bowl of extra-virgin olive oil and leave for a few hours to infuse the oil (the longer you can leave, it the stronger the flavours will be). Remove the garlic before using the oil

Honey Maple syrup

Milk Lactose-free milk, or almond, soy or rice milk

Mushroom Use lower FODMAP mushrooms, such as oyster mushrooms

Onion The best substitute is to use just the green parts of fresh spring onions (scallions), chives and leek (the dark green parts) or use some asafoetida powder, which you can find at health stores and online.

Pasta (wheat) Gluten-free pasta

Pistachio nuts Macadamia nuts, pecans or peanuts

Tomato (canned, fresh and paste) Avoid tinned tomatoes, which can be high in fructose, and instead use fresh tomatoes in your sauces, and leave out the garlic and sugar too. Secondly, do what Greeks call 'make it white', which means free of tomatoes and tomato-paste sauces. To get more flavour, use extra-virgin olive oil and fresh herbs instead.

Walnuts Pine nuts or macadamia nuts

Watermelon Rockmelon, grapefruit or honeydew

He has the most who is most content with the least.

– DIOGENES

Acknowledgements

There is no book without my parents: my mum, Sia, and my late father, Leo. My mum has given so much to make this book possible; she not only shared her incredible recipes but she opened up her home to make this book. For eight days and nights, side by side with me, my mum cooked nearly 90 dishes to be photographed. This is profound love and an enormous sacrifice that my mum made for me; this is the absolute boundless love of my mum. It's precious and I am so lucky. This is a love, care and sacrifice my mum has given to me every single day since she gave birth to me. She is a woman of such incredible purpose, strength and talent who taught me to be brave and believe in myself. My father's deep values, work ethic and love runs through me every day. My integrity and moral compass come from him. My dad taught me to always be proud of where you come from and to take people on their character and values, not on what they have or do. He taught me you can create beauty and hope anywhere. The spirit of my father is on every page of this book.

I am nothing without my family – they are my everything. My partner, Sarah, is my love, a joy and happiness that engulfs me, grounds me and makes me grateful to exist. Sarah inspires me to be optimistic, passionate and remain hopeful. I'm so proud of her for being the brilliant, loving, courageous and fearless person she is and for her passion to change the world, which I know she will.

My sister, Nola, has been my best friend since I was 12 years old. I'm so proud of her, the first Greek woman County Court judge in Australia. This is a testament to her towering talent. She is my champion, loyally in the ring by my side for more than three decades whenever life got too hard to face.

Nola and Sarah, along with Sia, Leo, Dan and Diana, are my heart, my joy, my sun, my sky, my true north and the foundation of my life. They give me the deepest love, hope and encouragement, and a place to truly call home. They always inspire me to be the best person I can be. I cannot imagine a day without them. I adore and love them more than life itself.

Thank you to my beautiful friends and relatives who came and helped me out for the group shoot and made the day so special. You bring so much happiness and joy to my life: Heidi, Peter, Gabriella, Nandini, Jana and her daughter Artemisia, and my uncle Nick and aunt Maria. Thank you also to all my beautiful friends who I could not physically squeeze around this cookbook table, for always creating a seat at the table for me in your lives. You are filitomo and philoxenia in action and I love you all.

I want to thank the movement and home of hope that is the Asylum Seeker Resource Centre and the community that makes it possible, from our staff, volunteers and board to our supporters. I feel privileged to be part of it and the vision of justice and welcome for refugees that it fearlessly stands for.

I want to thank the entire incredible Hardie Grant family for their belief in this book and their continuous support (Rushani Epa, Pam Brewster, Loran McDougall, Kristin Thomas, Celia Mance, Todd Rechner, Jessica Harvie, Kasi Collins, Madeleine Manifold and Sripali Edirisinghe). Thank you to Sarah Pannell for her gorgeous photography, Claire Pietersen for her amazing prep skills and encouragement, Deborah Kaloper for her beautiful food styling, Andy Warren for his terrific book design, Pru Engel for her brilliant and tireless work and support in editing our book, and Emily Stewart and Marg Bowman for proofreading.

Thank you to the Greek Australian community, too, for their encouragement and support. Thank you to those who offered to share family stories and photos of their grandparents and parents. I am so proud of my roots, my story and my culture and I hope this book makes you proud too.

I want to thank the fantastic Australian pottery community who rallied to donate pottery that we could use to display our home-cooked food to the public. Apologies that space limits meant I could not use everything donated for the shoot, but I want to thank you all here for the beauty and art you create: Anna Gianakis; Chloe Forder and Sea Salt Clay Studio (pages 81, 154, 200, 295, 302, salt bowl); Healesville Pottery (35, plate; 118, small bowl; 154, 200, olive bowl; 195, plate; 226, small plate; 263, small bowl; 267, plate); Ian (Ox) McColl and Oxart Pottery; Jade Lees-Pavey (17, 254, 200, 292, 295, 302, bread bowl; 17, 21, 154, 200, horta plate); Lisa Peri (21, olive oil bowl; 55, plates; 261, jug; 283, 294, 295, 302, spanakopita plate); Michelle J Cox (21, 154, 295, 200, 295, 302, feta plate; 51, plate; 59, plate; 130, brown plate; 154, 295, 200, broad beans and artichoke plate); Njalikwa Chongwe and Zinongo Gallery (219, bowl; 154, 295, zucchini salad bowl); Otti Made (130, speckled plate); Pauline Meade (4, bowl; 91, bowl; 118; large bowls; 154, 295, 283, Greek salad bowl); Penelope Duke (8, bowl; 17, 21, 154, 200, 295, tomato bowl; 35, bowl); Ratanak Ceramics (154, 283, 294, 295, toursi bowl); Sierra McManus; Stefanie Robinson (4, grey bowl; 17, 154, 200, 292, 295, 302, lemon bowl; 154, 283, 295, 302, grilled vegetable plate); Susie McIntosh (17, 98, 154, 200, pasta salad bowl, sweet pumpkin pastry plate; 81, plate); and Takewei Ceramics (154, 200, 295, marousalata plate; 241, plate). Thanks also to Femke Textiles (Linen tea towel, page 219).

Index

Published in 2023 by Hardie Grant Books,
an imprint of Hardie Grant Publishing

Hardie Grant Books (Melbourne)
Wurundjeri Country
Building 1, 658 Church Street
Richmond, Victoria 3121

Hardie Grant Books (London)
5th & 6th Floors
52–54 Southwark Street
London SE1 1UN

hardiegrant.com/books

Hardie Grant acknowledges the Traditional Owners of the Country
on which we work, the Wurundjeri People of the Kulin Nation and the
Gadigal People of the Eora Nation, and recognises their continuing
connection to the land, waters and culture. We pay our respects to their
Elders past and present.

A catalogue record for this
book is available from the
National Library of Australia

A Seat at My Table: Philoxenia
ISBN 978 1 74379 924 6

10 9 8 7 6 5 4 3 2 1

Commissioning Editor: Rushani Epa
Editor: Pru Engel
Design Manager: Kristin Thomas
Designer: Andy Warren
Typesetter: Megan Ellis
Photographer: Sarah Pannell
Prop Stylist: Deborah Kaloper
Home Economist: Claire Pietersen
Production Manager: Todd Rechner
Production Coordinator: Jessica Harvie

Colour reproduction by Splitting Image Colour Studio
Printed in China by Leo Paper Products LTD.